EDUCATION, CULTURE, AND POLITICS IN WEST GERMANY

SOCIETY, SCHOOLS, AND PROGRESS SERIES
General Editor: Professor Edmund J. King

OTHER TITLES IN THE SERIES

BARON, G.
Society, Schools, and Progress in England

CAMERON, J. and DODD, W. A.
Society, Schools, and Progress in Tanzania

CHIU-SAM TSANG
Society, Schools, and Progress in China

DIXON, C. W.
Society, Schools, and Progress in Scandinavia

FIGUEROA, J. J.
Society, Schools, and Progress in the West Indies

GRANT, N.
Society, Schools, and Progress in Eastern Europe

KATZ, J.
Society, Schools, and Progress in Canada

KING, E. J.
Society, Schools, and Progress in the U.S.A.

KLEINBERGER, A. F.
Society, Schools, and Progress in Israel

KOBAYASHI, T.
Society, Schools, and Progress in Japan

LEWIS, L. J.
Society, Schools, and Progress in Nigeria

PARTRIDGE, P. H.
Society, Schools, and Progress in Australia,
Australian revised edition

PAULSTON, R. G.
Society, Schools, and Progress in Peru

SARGENT, J.
Society, Schools, and Progress in India

For other titles of interest please see the end of this book

The terms of our inspection copy service apply to all
the above books. Full details of all books listed will
gladly be sent upon request.

2116^{2151}

EDUCATION, CULTURE, AND POLITICS IN WEST GERMANY

BY

ARTHUR HEARNDEN

London University Institute of Education

$\frac{379}{-43}$

PERGAMON PRESS

OXFORD · NEW YORK · TORONTO
SYDNEY · PARIS · FRANKFURT

U. K.   Pergamon Press Ltd., Headington Hill Hall,
                 Oxford OX3 0BW, England
U. S. A.   Pergamon Press Inc., Maxwell House, Fairview Park,
                 Elmsford, New York 10523, U.S.A.
C A N A D A   Pergamon of Canada Ltd., P.O. Box 9600,
                 Don Mills M3C 2T9, Ontario, Canada
A U S T R A L I A   Pergamon Press (Aust.) Pty. Ltd., 19a Boundary
                 Street, Rushcutters Bay, N.S.W. 2011, Australia
F R A N C E   Pergamon Press SARL, 24 rue des Ecoles,
                 75240 Paris, Cedex 05, France
W E S T   G E R M A N Y   Pergamon Press GmbH, 6242 Kronberg-Taunus,
                 Pferdstrasse 1, Frankfurt-am-Main, West Germany

First edition 1976

Library of Congress Cataloging in Publication Data

Hearnden, Arthur.
Education, culture, and politics in West Germany.

(Society schools, and progress series) (Pergamon
international library of science, technology, engineering,
and social studies)
Bibliography: p.
Includes index.
1. Education and state--Germany, West. I. Title.
LC93.G4H392 1975   379.43   75-35529
ISBN 0-08-019916-X
ISBN 0-08-019915-1 flexi

Printed in Great Britain by A. Wheaton & Co., Exeter

Contents

Author's Note

This book was written at the invitation of Professor Edmund King of King's College, London, and was intended to take its place alongside the many other titles that have already appeared in the "Society, Schools and Progress" series. While it remains part of this series, the title has been changed to *Education, Culture, and Politics in West Germany,* which I believe gives a truer indication of its main areas of interest.

CHAPTER 1

The Federal Republic

The Federal Republic of Germany, West Germany, is obviously enough a remnant of an earlier entity. Its juxtaposition with the German Democratic Republic, East Germany, implies that Hitler's Reich was split in two after the Second World War. Consequently it is sometimes forgotten that for many years after its creation, the East German State, the *DDR*, was referred to in the West as *Mitteldeutschland* (Middle Germany), a deliberate reminder that a third large territory of the pre-war Reich, to the east of the rivers Oder and Neisse, was placed under the administration of Poland and the Soviet Union according to the terms of the Potsdam Agreement of 1945.

It has been difficult for Germans to accept this tripartite division of the Reich. Generations of schoolchildren were taught to regard its unification under Bismarck in 1871 as the ordained climax of German history. Some hundred years later it was for many a bitter pill when in 1970 the loss of the eastern territories was formally acknowledged and then, in 1972 agreement was reached on a general relations treaty between the Federal and Democratic Republics. The consequences of the Second World War are therefore perpetuated in a division which now appears as permanent as any such demarcation in history can be. The fact that such recognition was possible after a quarter of a century of mutual suspicion and rivalry emphasises how much more secure and self-confident both countries have become, a development that was confirmed by the admission of both of them to the United Nations in 1973. In the 1950s West Germany achieved a remarkable recovery, the "economic miracle" which gave it a leading position, industrially and commercially, in western Europe. Though less publicised, the recovery of the East German State in the 1960s was hardly less spectacular, and has earned for it what is probably the highest living standard in the Eastern bloc. Both Germanies are rich and powerful States. But they are still, despite the treaty, wary of one another, fearing ideological infiltration. It is as well to bear in mind the resulting frontier mentality, especially in Berlin, when the institutions of West Germany are examined.

THE ANTECEDENCE OF CULTURAL FEDERALISM

There has long been a connection between national aspirations and education in Germany. The defeat of Prussia at the hands of Napoleon in 1806 was a humiliation aggravated by the subsequent fragmentation of Prussian territory. The resulting rancour expressed itself not only in a desire to revive Prussian fortunes but in an awareness both in this and in other German States of the weakness that their disunity had brought on the Germanic peoples in general. It was in such a context that the philosopher Fichte delivered a series of lectures in the winter of 1807-8, the *Addresses to the German People*, in which he passionately affirmed the importance of education in furthering the cause of German unity. A prominent theme of the *Addresses* was that Germany was not a State but a nation, and, furthermore, one which deserved to be pre-eminent in Europe by virtue of its superior civilisation; for Fichte the German language and literature were the finest in Europe. His theme was readily taken up, since it gave expression to the growing desire to break free of the French culture which had hitherto greatly influenced intellectual life in Germany.

While the educational reforms carried through by Wilhelm von Humboldt between 1808 and 1810 which are discussed in more detail in the next chapter played a significant part in the rebuilding of Prussia, the desire for unity of the German people as a whole remained unsatisfied. The settlement which brought the Napoleonic wars to a close in 1815 perpetuated the autonomy of the individual State rulers; and they, unwilling to sacrifice their independence, tended to look askance at manifestations of the national movement. The ideal persisted, however, and in the united Germany that was envisaged by the liberal elements, education was regarded as a potential unifying agent. The constitution drafted by the self-appointed Frankfurt Assembly of 1848 included a demand for a central Ministry of Education to promote the improvement and standardisation of the various State provisions. After the failure of the liberal revolution, however, the eventual unification under Bismarck was achieved quite independently of such aspirations. Educational development continued to depend on the initiative of the individual rulers, though the influence of the Prussian model did spread to a number of other States. The idea of a central authority responsible for education throughout Germany was not again seriously entertained until the establishment of the Weimar Republic after the First World War. Under the terms of the Constitution of 1919 a new cultural department was set up in the federal Ministry of the Interior, and a Commission was formed in which representatives of both federal and *Land* administrations were to collaborate in working towards a national policy. The one permanent achievement of this co-operation was the passing of the law which abolished private primary education and made the four primary years of the *Volkschule* the standard beginning for all children. This was a significant step, for, though a small number of the private schools did survive, it was no longer common practice to have a very specific preparation in such institutions for entry to the *Gymnasium* or grammar school at the age of 9, a privileged route by comparison with what was accessible to the great majority of the school population. At this time, therefore, the basis of the modern system was established.

Little else, however, was achieved in the domain of full-time education. The pattern of German politics made it difficult to bring about more far-reaching changes. Those coalitions that were prepared to do so were minority governments lacking the power to see controversial legislation through to its conclusion. The more broadly based coalition governments did perhaps have the required strength, but their composition was too disparate to permit agreement. The advocates of an all-embracing State system – broadly speaking the Socialist and Communist groupings – were at the same time in favour of the abolition of confessional schools. This was totally unacceptable to the conservative Centre Party and its associate, the Bavarian People's Party, both of which had strong links with the Catholic Church. Therefore, despite the efforts of the Commission to devise plans for a single national school system, corresponding legislation was out of the question. Once again the development of schools was left to the individual *Länder* of which at this time there were eighteen. Within these there were various reform initiatives designed to modify the sharp dualism between the academic *Gymnasium* sector and the remainder, and even, in the case of Thuringia, to set up a complete comprehensive system. As a result of this variety there was at the end of the Weimar period a greater proliferation of types of school than there had been at the beginning.[1]

From 1933 on it was the central theme of Nazi education policy to impose unity on this diversity. A central ministry was created to achieve this headed by a former unemployed teacher and long-standing Party member. There was some justification for reorganising the system. Its complications created problems for families who migrated from one region to another, and the frequent transfer of officials was a notable feature of the Nazi administration.[2] But the principal motive was ideological. A passage from *Mein Kampf* illustrates Hitler's intention to make of the school system an instrument for the inculcation of Nazi ideology:

"The whole end of education in a people's State, and its crown, is found by burning into the heart and brain of the youth entrusted to it an instinctive and comprehended sense of race. ... It is the duty of a national State to see to it that a history of the world is eventually written in which the question of race shall occupy a predominant position. ... According to this plan the curriculum must be built up with this point of view. According to this education must be so arranged that the young person leaving school is not half pacifist, democrat, or what you will, but a complete German."[3]

To achieve these ends the content of the curriculum was transformed and pressure put on recalcitrant members of the teaching profession to induce them to subscribe to the tenets of National Socialism.

The administrative measures taken involved firstly the final abolition of the remaining private primary schools. This ensured that the entire school population could begin its education on a common basis and in accordance with the official ideology. At the secondary level, which was for the Nazis of secondary importance, the type of school that was most highly valued was the *Deutsche Oberschule*, a Prussian creation of the 1920s designed to specialise in specifically German culture rather than the classics which was

---

[1] For a detailed account of educational policy during the Weimar Republic see Christoph Führ, *Zur Schulpolitik der Weimarer Republik*, Weinheim, 1972.

[2] Cf. R. H. Samuel and R. Hinton Thomas, *Education and Society in Modern Germany*, London, 1949, p. 50.

[3] Translation in Erika Mann, *School for Barbarians*, London, 1939, p. 40.

still strong in the *Gymnasium*. Indeed, the *Gymnasium* was severely restricted in its scope, the duration of its course was reduced by a year, a
reduction by an additional year was planned, and the generally anti-
intellectual approach to the educational system was emphasised by the
active discouragement of university studies. The new élite sector was
constituted by the boarding schools specially set up by the Party, the
National Political Educational Institutions (*Nationalpolitische Erziehungs-
anstalten*), the Adolf Hitler Schools, and the German Boarding Schools
(*Deutsche Heimschulen*). It need hardly be emphasised that all three
categories vividly illustrated the Nazi conception of education. How much
of all this was disapproved of at the time by the general public and how
much was endorsed is an unanswerable question. Certain it is, however,
that in the post-war period the memories of what had happened after 1933
reinforced the older tradition of aversion to central control of education.

THE *LÄNDER* OF THE FEDERATION

Though in the early stages of the occupation period the Western Allies
were in their different ways eager to influence the development of
education in their respective zones, they gradually came to accept that this
was a field in which it was desirable for the Germans themselves to have
the main say in determining policy. The effect of first involving leading
Germans in the reorganisation of schools and later of giving provincial
assemblies the right to legislate on educational matters was, as indicated
earlier, to reinstate the tradition of regional responsibility after the
centralisation which had been introduced in the Third Reich and had left
such a bitter taste. When the Federal Republic was created in 1949 its
constitution or "Basic Law" consolidated this tradition by leaving
educational legislation to the individual *Länder*. At this point it is appropriate to make a brief survey of these components of the federation.

On the creation of the Federal Republic in 1949 those territories which
in the immediate post-war period were administered by the Western Allies,
the United Kingdom, the USA, and France, were grouped to form eleven
constituent States, *Länder*, each with its own legislature. The smallest such
Land is Bremen, which consists of the cities of Bremen and Bremerhaven
and the area immediately surrounding them. An important shipping
centre, Bremen was in the immediate post-war period an island of United

6   Education, Culture, and Politics in West Germany

States administration in the British zone of occupation. The other "city state", Hamburg, is West Germany's largest port and commercial centre with an independent tradition deriving from its membership of the medieval Hanseatic League. The northernmost *Land* is Schleswig-Holstein, the borders of which include stretches of the North Sea and Baltic coasts and the frontier with Denmark. It has traditionally depended largely on agriculture, but has important shipping centres in the capital Kiel and in Lübeck and Flensburg, and its share of industry has been increasing. After the war it was in these three northern *Länder* that the radical impulse to change the educational system was strongest, the left-wing parties being well represented in all three legislative assemblies.

In addition to Hamburg and Schleswig-Holstein, the British zone of occupation included the two large *Länder* of North Rhine-Westphalia and Lower Saxony. At the heart of the former is the vast industrial complex of the Ruhr, the power-house of the economic recovery. An agglomeration of cities in and near the Ruhr, which includes Cologne, Essen, the *Land* capital Düsseldorf, and the federal capital Bonn, makes North Rhine-Westphalia the most populous *Land* with some 17 million inhabitants, roughly equivalent to the population of the *DDR*. Beyond the perimeter of the industrialised area is the rich agricultural land of the lower Rhine valley and the plains of Westphalia. Lower Saxony, in area the second largest *Land*, extends from the frontier with the *DDR* in the east to the Dutch border in the west. It is a composite made up of a number of formerly separate provinces one of which bore the name of the present capital Hanover. Consequently it embraces a wide variety of traditions, not least those of the many refugees from the east which it had to absorb. Only Schleswig-Holstein took in proportionately more refugees than Lower Saxony.

Apart from Bremen the *Länder* administered by the Americans were Hesse, Bavaria, and part of what is now Baden-Württemberg. Hesse, lying in the heart of Germany, has vast forests and picturesque towns that retain many of their medieval exteriors. The *Land* capital is the spa of Wiesbaden. Also in Hesse is Frankfurt, one of Germany's premier industrial, commercial, communications centres and the birthplace of Goethe. Since the war political activity has in this *Land* taken on a fairly radical character with the *SPD* strongly represented in the Assembly, a situation which has been reflected in efforts to reorganise the school system on more egalitarian principles than before. The growing number of comprehensive schools has been a recent feature of education in Hesse. The opposite tradition of staunch conservatism has been evident in Bavaria, territorially the largest *Land*, covering one-third of the entire Federal Republic, and with a daunting reputation for independence if not downright intransigence. Such attitudes are rooted in the long history of a region that was scarcely affected by the Reformation. Some three-quarters of the inhabitants are Roman Catholics, a factor which greatly influences political structures: since the war the *CSU*, sister party to the federal *CDU*, has dominated the legislative assembly. However, the general impression conveyed of stolid and unimaginative conservatism is belied by the *Land* capital Munich, a cosmopolitan city, foremost as a centre for the arts and a mecca for the unconventional. The beauty of its mountains, lakes, and forests makes Bavaria the most magnetic region for tourists in the Federal Republic.

If Bavaria leads in tourism, Baden-Württemberg is not far behind, containing as it does the Black Forest, the Swabian Jura, and the ancient university towns of Heidelberg, Tübingen, and Freiburg. With further universities at the capital Stuttgart, Karlsruhe, Mannheim, Hohenheim, Ulm, and Konstanz, Baden-Württemberg is more generously provided with university education than any of the other *Länder*. Recent decades have seen this region experience rapid industrial development so that it is now second only to North Rhine-Westphalia in economic and financial strength. The political tradition has been conservative with the *CDU* generally the strongest party; in their education policies the *Land* governments have generally taken a positive if cautious attitude to experiment and innovation. To the west of the Rhine is Rhineland-Palatinate which together with parts of Baden-Württemberg formed the French zone during the Occupation. Mainz is the capital of this major wine-growing region which has, like Bavaria, a predominantly Roman Catholic population and exhibits on the whole a similar political conservatism. Also on the western border of the federation, but further to the south, is the Saar, the small but rich industrial area which declined to accept the eventual integration into France that was planned for it after the war and as a result of a referendum became part of the Federal Republic in 1957.

Berlin, the old Reich capital, was placed under the joint administration of the four Allies after the war, and was the meeting ground for East and

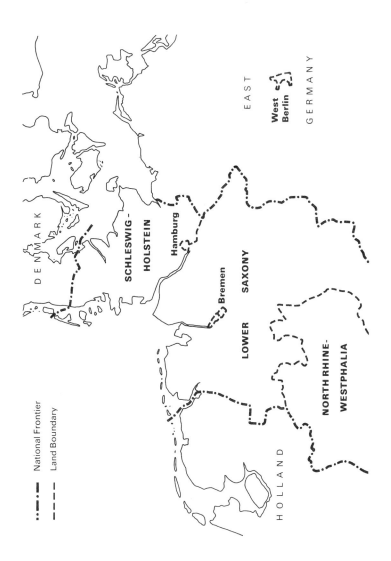

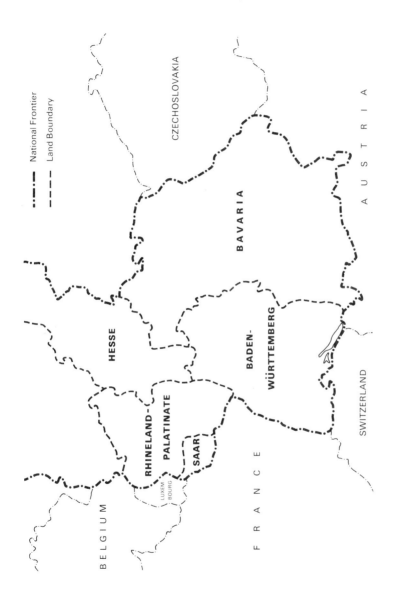

West until the building of the Wall in 1961. Now the former Russian sector of the city is the capital of the *DDR*, while the remaining sectors constitute the special political entity of West Berlin. For practical purposes West Berlin is part of the Federal Republic. But its beleaguered situation has made it difficult to attract new industry and give it a vigorous and self-sufficient economy, and it remains dependent on financial subsidies from West Germany proper. Its political traditions reflect the strength of both the Christian Democrats and the *SPD*, with the latter recently in the ascendant. The school system still retains a good many of the new features that resulted from the radical changes introduced during the period of four-power control.

THE POST-WAR DEVELOPMENT OF CULTURAL FEDERALISM

Though education was left to the individual *Länder*, the Federal Constitution of 1949 laid down guidelines in which were enshrined certain important general principles. The relevant articles are couched in the fairly general terms that are customary in such documents. The initial ones uphold the dignity of man, his inalienable rights, equality before the law, and the free development of personality provided that there is neither infringement of the rights of others nor offence against the moral code. Discrimination on grounds of sex, descent, race, language, social origin and background, religious, political, or other beliefs is proscribed, and freedom of worship and conscience guaranteed. Specific support is accorded to marriage and the family, and the care and upbringing of children is declared to be the natural right of parents and their primary duty. It is at this point that these general principles begin to impinge on more specifically educational issues. For when the existence of confessional schools has in the post-war period appeared to be an obstacle to the development and expansion of the educational system, these schools have defended themselves on the constitutional grounds of the parents' right to choose them. Such an issue can become inflamed when, for example, a reorganisation scheme requires the merging of the senior classes of several elementary schools, perhaps of different denominations, in order to form a new secondary school.

The five sections of Article 7, which is specifically concerned with the school system, are worded as follows:

"(1) The entire school system is under the supervision of the State.

"(2) Parents or guardians have the right to make such decisions as may be necessary regarding the participation of children in religious instruction.

"(3) In State schools, religious instruction is a normal school subject unless the school is specifically secular. Regardless of the State's right of supervision, religious instruction is given in accordance with the principles of the religious communities. No teacher may be compelled to give religious instruction against his or her will.

"(4) The right to set up private schools is guaranteed. Private schools as a replacement for State schools require the authorisation of the State authorities and must conform to the *Land* laws. This authorisation is to be given if the private schools do not fall behind the standards of the State schools in their objectives and their equipment and facilities, as well as in the academic qualifications of their teaching staff, and so long as segregation of schoolchildren on the basis of family means is not encouraged. The authorisation is to be withheld if the economic and legal position of the teachers is not sufficiently safeguarded.

"(5) A private primary school is only permissible if the authorities recognise that a special pedagogical interest is involved or if, in response to the requests of parents, it is to be set up as a community, denominational, or secular school, where a State school of this kind does not exist."

A further article states that "all Germans have the right to choose their profession or trade, their place of work, and training establishment". This is another item capable of giving rise to controversy in the context of the growing need for restrictions on entry to higher education. The introduction of a *numerus clausus* has in fact, as will be discussed in a later chapter, been challenged at the federal constitutional court in Karlsruhe.

Provided that they did not infringe these various principles, however, the *Länder* were left to get on with the task of planning and running their individual school systems. Consequently education aroused very little interest at federal level. Debates on the subject in the *Bundestag,* the lower house of the federal legislative assembly, were comparatively rare and poorly attended. Even if this body had wished to assume greater responsibility, its ability to do so would have been constrained by the powers of the upper house, the *Bundesrat*. This body, made up of representatives of the *Land* governments, has the function of protecting their interests and would not have acquiesced in any attempt to impose a co-ordinated, national education policy on them. Symptomatic of this situation was the absence of any federal Ministry of Education in the early post-war years and the rejection in 1956 of a suggestion that one should be set up.

However, the *Länder* could clearly not operate in total isolation from one another. Co-operation, at least in certain administrative matters, was essential, and there were also policy issues in which they were inter-dependent. The agency through which this co-operation took place was the Conference of Education Ministers (*Kultusministerkonferenz*) which after informal beginnings during the Occupation period soon acquired a secretariat in Bonn and developed into the major forum for the ventila-tion of national issues in education. During the 1950s these were related mainly to the problems of achieving some standardisation of the diverg-ing practices of the *Länder*. These, in fact, caused a variety of problems, particularly in the case of families moving from one *Land* to another. Academic and professional qualifications were not necessarily mutually recognised, school curricula varied, e.g. in respect of the foreign languages that were obligatory, and various administrative discrepancies such as the timing of the school year were additional irritants. Much of this was pro-gressively tidied up through the work of the *Kultusministerkonferenz*, culminating in the Düsseldorf Agreement of 1955 to which all *Länder* except Bavaria were signatories. In its decisions the conference therefore concentrated on pragmatic solutions to immediate problems.

Consideration of the more far-reaching issues became the province of a special commission, the *Deutscher Ausschuss für das Erziehungs- und Bildungswesen,* set up in 1953 on the joint initiative of the *Kultusminister-konferenz* and the federal Ministry of the Interior. Its task was to produce recommendations for the reshaping of the entire educational provision of the Federal Republic, independently of any political, administrative, or interest group pressure. Particularly significant among the more informed groups among which priorities of national policy were discussed was the so-called *Ettlinger Kreis,* a group of businessmen and educationists who met regularly in Ettlingen near Karlsruhe and published the results of their deliberations in a series of booklets. Both these and the early recommendations of the *Deutscher Ausschuss* began to arouse some misgivings about the state of the German educational system, and a climax was reached when the *Ausschuss* produced its controversial outline plan (*Rahmenplan*) in 1959, a document which will be discussed in detail in a later chapter.

The debate sparked off by the *Rahmenplan* created a new awareness of educational problems at a national level. The *Kultusministerkonferenz* acted promptly on its less conventional elements — the raising of the school-leaving age to 15, the refinement of selection procedures, and the reorganisation of the upper secondary curricula which had become heavily overloaded — but took no collective decision on the more controversial one of the postponement of the age of selection, which would in effect have been a first and very modest step towards the establishment of a comprehensive system. Interest died down again but was sharply revived by the publication of a book called *The German Educational Catastrophe* (*Die Deutsche Bildungskatastrophe*) by Georg Picht, somewhat extravagantly predicting economic disaster if the reorganisation of the system was not pursued with urgency. The fresh debate that followed this publication brought home the ineffectiveness of a body like the *Deutscher Ausschuss*, whose terms of reference were solely advisory, and set in motion negotiations which led to the creation of its successor the *Deutscher Bildungsrat* (German Education Council). The intention was that this body should be in a much stronger position to promote a national education policy. One of its two committees included the political representation which was necessary to ensure that its proposals were realistic. The interest in comprehensive planning of educational development had thus greatly advanced the cause of a national system for the whole of West Germany.

But the task facing the *Bildungsrat* remained a delicate one, for any recommendations it made still had to be accepted by the *Land* governments. With coercion ruled out, a strategy of persuasion was necessary, and the federal government was constantly at pains to affirm that it was, as Chancellor Erhardt put it, "certainly not motivated by the desire to contest the competence of the *Länder* in regard to educational policy". None the less, the desire of the central government to play a more important role in education was evidenced by the expansion of the former federal Ministry of Scientific Research to become the Ministry of Education and Science in 1969. It is a measure of how much attitudes had changed since 1956 that it was now possible to put through the amendment to the Constitution which this innovation required. The next step in central–regional co-operation was the creation of the *Bund-Länder-Kommission*, the federal-*Land* commission for educational planning. In 1973 this body presented its comprehensive plan for the period up to 1985, the *Bildungsgesamtplan*.

CONTROL, ADMINISTRATION, AND PARTICIPATION

However important the growth of co-operation between federal and *Land* authorities, it should be acknowledged that it represents a level of policy-making far removed from the great majority of decisions affecting the day-to-day affairs of individual schools. While the general framework of education policy may well be of concern to many teachers and parents, their more immediate preoccupations tend to be with its practical implications, the provision of adequate buildings, and the sanctioning of expenditure for new equipment – in short the service which the schools provide for their immediate locality. In these matters where decision-making relates to the disbursement of public funds, there are three main levels among which responsibility is distributed, the *Land* Education Ministry, the local authority which is sometimes organised on a two-tier – district and commune – basis and the individual school. The problem is the eternal one of finding the right degree of decentralisation. Excessive concentration of power at the level of the Ministry can stifle any incentive to innovate in individual schools, since the obligation to follow strict regulations must discourage initiative among individual teachers. Yet however much schools demand the right to run their own affairs there are clearly limits to the autonomy they can be allowed. Their activities must be co-ordinated. The role of the district and commune authorities is important as mediator between claims which can represent unacceptable extremes of control or freedom.

Though there are certain variations of detail among the *Länder* there is, in principle, a fairly clear delineation of powers. The *Land* authorities are responsible for the specifically educational aspects of the service, the structure of the system, the curricula that are to be followed, and the appointment and payment of teachers. The local authorities, on the other hand, are responsible for all aspects of material provision, the construction and maintenance of buildings, and the equipment of individual schools.

Responsibility relates to finance, but the separation of financial obligations is not quite so clear-cut. The *Land* authorities subsidise the running costs incurred by the local authorities in two main ways. The first is by direct intervention to help finance specific building or equipment programmes. The second involves indirect help through a system designed to equalise the spending power of local authorities by subsidising the less prosperous communities and thus ensuring a reasonably uniform standard of provision of local services. Since this subsidy, which would correspond to the rate support grant in England and Wales, is not exclusively for education, its effect on the provision of schools can vary greatly. In the reverse direction there are some *Länder* in which the local authorities supplement the finance provided centrally, generally by raising specific school taxes as a contribution towards the payment of teachers.

This complexity makes it difficult to identify the relative degree of financial support for education emanating from the two main sources. However, the general trend would appear to be a marked growth in the share of expenditure borne by the *Land* and a corresponding decline in the share borne by the local authority. This in turn may well reflect a similar centralising trend at a higher level, for an obvious concomitant of the establishment of federal bodies, such as the *Bildungsrat*, the new federal Ministry, and the *Bund-Länder-Kommission* is a greater readiness on the part of the federal government to subsidise the education expenditure of the individual *Länder*. It is a development which is easily understandable in the context of the rising costs that accompany rising expectations.

In view of the fact that Germany has in the past displayed a marked predilection for bureaucratic control in the social services, the tendency towards centralisation of provision of finance has been a cause for concern. The *Strukturplan* of 1970 recognised this concern and pointed to the need to give heads of individual schools more room for manoeuvre in expenditure if a healthy development was to be encouraged: "[as part of the plan] the individual educational institutions acquire greater independence and at the same time feature more prominently in the rationalised order of priorities which is the outcome of the total planning." In any such exercise designed to counterbalance the increased powers that are tending to accrue to *Land* ministers, the potential losers are the local authorities, which can become merely agencies for the channelling of funds with a decreasing say in how they should be spent. The problem greatly exercised the *Bildungsrat* in the years following the issue of the *Strukturplan*, for it was essential to arrive at some agreed delineation of powers and responsibilities that would meet the aspirations of those involved at all three levels of *Land*, local authority, and individual school. The first report on the subject stated in somewhat repetitious fashion:

"Increased independence of individual schools means in the context of State and local administration a transfer of responsibility to the individual school. Within this framework schools should act and make decisions independently. The increased individual responsibility of the school requires that teachers, pupils, and parents should share it. Such participation only makes sense if the school is given its own responsibility. Increased independence takes account of the fact that the complex procedures involved in school teaching cannot be predetermined down to the last detail. The participation of those involved takes account of the fact that an institution cannot make decisions and act on them independently of the people who are involved in its activities. Through participation the common responsibility and cooperation of teachers, pupils, and parents in the social system known as school should be made possible and strengthened. The collective shaping of the school should be institutionally guaranteed and laid down for the individual domains."[4]

Thus the question of how the various parties in the administrative hierarchy should interact with one another touches on the concept of participation which has attracted increasing attention since de Gaulle made so much of it as a panacea for social unrest. It is a concept that invites scepticism: a speaker at a Cambridge Union Society debate described it as "that ultimate in Gaullist mysticism". Chimeric or not, however, it is a notion that set in train an extensive series of administrative changes in France and which has ramified widely in discussions of educational policy in Germany.

At the heart of the matter is the view that education must more and more be seen as part of its social environment. This idea is not entirely to be dismissed as a statement of the obvious, for it has been clear in the past that the provision of schools has not always been sensibly planned to fit into the wider pattern of general urban and rural development. For this

4 Deutscher Bildungsrat, *Zur Reform von Organisation und Verwaltung im Bildungswesen*, Teil I, Stuttgart, 1973, p. 17.

reason the threatened erosion of local authority powers in education is viewed with some apprehension, for it is the local authority that is best placed to assess needs and direct the response to them. Thus it is argued that it is important for the local authority to be deeply involved in the running of its own schools, and this is seen as an important dimension of the idea of participation.

But if the community must be involved with the school, it is equally important that the school should identify with the community. Where formerly it conducted its activities in sequestered seclusion, it is now held to have an obligation to open its doors and lay bare its workings to the world outside. And to be able to do this, it is argued, it must itself be a reasonably democratic, participating community. Much of the criticism of pre-war German schools was directed at their authoritarian tradition. Those who reacted against this – Froebel, for example, or Wyneken – by pioneering a more democratic way of going about things, were always a small minority swimming against the tide. In the post-war period, especially at the instigation of the United States occupation forces, strenuous efforts were made to establish a measure of pupil participation in school administration (*Schülermitverwaltung*) in the belief that democratic processes in the school would act as a leaven in a society where authoritarian traditions still retained a strong hold. Recent discussions on the theme of participation have once again focused attention on this aspect of German school life.

A democratic form of school government does not alone forge direct links with the community, however; potentially the most effective agency for this is the parents. Particularly in the *Gymnasium* sector there is a healthy tradition of parental interest in academic progress at school. Periodic meetings are held at which teachers discuss their pupils' progress with parents. Provision is made, too, for parents individually to consult subject teachers who generally set aside one or more periods a week for visits of this kind – the *Sprechstunde*. The extent to which parents avail themselves of this opportunity is, of course, variable, as is the attitude which individual teachers take to it. None the less, it is a formal recognition of the professional role of teachers in this respect.

Perhaps the most difficult problem in the matter of parent participation derives from the long-established practice as regards homework. Traditionally the school day has been confined to the morning hours, say from 7·45 to 1·15: children then go home for lunch and are expected to spend a good deal of the afternoon at their homework. Furthermore, parents are expected to help with this and sometimes virtually to assess it. The advantages for the pupils from the more educated family backgrounds are obvious, and it is hardly surprising that surveys have shown that a positive attitude to school is much more prevalent in the middle class than the working class.[5] It should be emphasised once again that a positive attitude is anything but a nebulous concept since it involves so much in the way of active supervision.

Such findings have sharpened awareness of the need, firstly, to consider schooling on an all-day basis, and secondly, to involve and encourage those parents who are apathetic or intimidated by the aura of school. For the first, a good many experiments are in hand, and it would certainly seem that there are the beginnings of a movement among teachers actively to espouse the second course. This is particularly true of the more experimental and innovative schools where there tends to be a need to rely on parental support. On the other side there are indications of the growing concern about education among parents as a whole, e.g. the emergence of periodicals especially concerned with parents' interests. Increased provision of education, too, has led to an increase in the proportion of parents who are confident enough to take an active interest.

In turn this increasing interest appears to have brought to light some dissatisfaction with the formal provision made for parental participation. This dissatisfaction derives from the reluctance of the teaching profession to grant parents a major say in matters which directly affect the teacher's professional performance. The latter do not expect to be told how to do their job any more than would lawyers or oxyacetylene welders. But since education provides such lush pastures for the lay dabbler, the teacher's particular professional expertise is always more likely to come under critical scrutiny than that of practitioners in other less accessible fields. The core of the conflict is, then, the question of how far and in what precise ways the participation of parents can be formalised in order to effect a reconciliation between the demands of decentralisation of authority and promotion of grass-roots democracy, on the one hand, and protection of the esoterism of teaching against violation on the part of the

5 Cf. H. Peisert and R. Dahrendorf, *Der vorzeitige Abgang vom Gymnasium*, Kultusministerium Baden-Württemberg, 1968, p. 86.

uninitiated, on the other. What is required is the creation of institutions that can impose on a potentially conflict-laden situation the conditions under which constructive co-operation between the two sides can thrive.

The most important formal grouping to represent parents is the *Bundeselternrat* which was formed in 1952 through the merging of eighteen smaller organisations. Since 1968 this body has spoken for parents of all *Länder* in the federation. It is influential enough to have dealings at a high level with such policy-making bodies as the federal ministry and the *Bund-Länder-Kommission*. It has, for example, been particularly active in the deliberations over the revision of the upper secondary school examination system and the requirements for admission to universities. Other groupings represent more specialised interests, e.g. those of religious bodies or of individual types of school or of particular professions with an interest in the way educational policy affects their recruitment. Throughout the range of these groupings is a predictably strong tendency to over-representation of the middle class and of parents with a high level of aspiration. Indeed, the movement as a whole is some-times seen as a conspiracy to preserve a meritocratic *status quo*: in Hesse, for example, where the comprehensive school movement is strongly supported by some groups of teachers, parents' organisations are largely hostile to it and have been criticised by some teachers' unions for undemocratic procedures.[6]

The issues affecting parent participation therefore touch on fundamental problems of the workings of democracy. It can be argued that the importance of this kind of lay involvement increases in proportion to the growth of centralisation in decision-making. But such involvement can well lead to an increase in confrontation. Here a number of factors already adumbrated are relevant, not least the need to strengthen the professional expertise and confidence of teachers in a country where in-service training facilities have not been highly developed. But whatever the ways in which general conditions can be improved, whatever the resources that can be poured into the schools to meet the criticisms, the resolution of conflicts between opposed groups is in the last analysis a pragmatic exercise in taking account of the circumstances of each individual case.

---

[6] Klaus Schleicher, *Elternhaus und Schule*, Düsseldorf, 1972, p. 27.

CHAPTER 2

Traditions in Education: Thinkers and Practitioners

Many elements go to make up the distinctive culture that finds its expression in German schools. There are, moreover, a number of ways of exploring this culture in order to explain how it differs from that of other European countries. One of these is to see it from the perspective of the succession of major personalities who have left their mark upon it, an approach which in the present context is more than usually fruitful in that Germany has had more than its share of "great educators". Among them there are several whose names stand out like beacons: Humboldt, the virtual creator of the *Gymnasium* of modern times; Kerschensteiner, the pioneer of German vocational education; Froebel, whose influence on pre-school and primary education stretched far beyond Germany. In the brief account that follows the choice among the many other prominent figures of the nineteenth and twentieth centuries is inevitably somewhat limited and arbitrary. However, the hope is that it will be possible to compress into a short space enough to provide an elementary explanation of the traditions that have greatly influenced the development of education in the post-war period as well as those which have not shown such durability. A convenient starting-point is the revival of the *Gymnasium* in the early nineteenth century, one of the great educational achievements of Humboldt.

THE NEOCLASSICISM OF HUMBOLDT

Wilhelm von Humboldt was born at Potsdam in 1767. Following a family tradition he entered the public service and held a number of government appointments at home and diplomatic posts abroad. In the brief period from December 1808 to June 1810, during which he was responsible for education, his impact on the Prussian school system was remarkable. The *Gymnasien*, or grammar schools, had been in decline, in many cases abandoned by the aristocracy in favour of academies which were considered to fulfil their requirements more effectively. Under Humboldt they enjoyed a resurgence which left them unchallenged as institutions for the secondary education of the future leaders of society. Humboldt's conception of the aims of *Gymnasium* education, even if it was subsequently interpreted in a way other than he intended, has had an influence that is still felt today.

The nature of this conception is partly explained by the personality and interests of Humboldt himself. He was a scholar of wide interests embracing history, literature, philosophy, political theory and philology, and his many writings in these fields reveal him as no dilettante but one of the foremost intellects of his time. Above all he was a Hellenist, participating in the glorification of ancient Greece which permeated much of German literature in the late eighteenth century. The opening paragraph of his essay on the Greek character (*Von dem griechischen Charakter überhaupt und der idealischen Ansicht desselben insbesondere*) is an eloquent panegyric which aptly conveys the starting-point in his thinking:

"Modern times and antiquity are entirely foreign to one another. We see in the Greeks a nation in whose fortunate hands everything which deep down we know to embody what is highest and richest in human existence had already reached final maturity. To us they represent a race made of nobler and purer stuff. The centuries when they were in their prime are for us a time in which nature emerged fresher from the workshop of creation, and with no adulteration of its perfection. Scarcely looking ahead or behind them, the Greeks planted and founded everything afresh. Following their own impulses in pure simplicity and giving expression to their natural aspirations, they created models of eternal beauty and greatness."

The literary and artistic works on ancient Greece thus appeared to Humboldt as unrivalled peaks of intellectual and aesthetic achievement, and an understanding of this idealised epoch was for him a primary aim of education. In this search for understanding, the scholarship involved in piecing together the history of an earlier civilisation was only subsidiary. The most significant task was to comprehend the ideal of fully rounded human development which the Greeks symbolised.

For Humboldt the specific goal of education was to realise this ideal in the schools and universities of his own day. The cardinal medium was, naturally enough, the classics, and in the *Gymnasium* of the nineteenth century they experienced a revival such as has not been seen since. But the study of the classics was a means to an end, namely the education of the individual in all spheres of knowledge. As conveyed by the term *Bildung,* or *Allgemeinbildung,* education, or general education, was equated with the cultivation of a wide variety of interests, of sophisticated intellectual and aesthetic standards. But it should be borne in mind that this poly-mathic view did not merely imply an accumulation of knowledge passed on from teacher to pupil. The striving towards the ideal was a matter for the individual; a necessary condition for the acquisition of *Bildung* was the individual's own desire to cultivate the intellect and the aesthetic sense to the highest degree possible. Humboldt acknowledged that this could only be the genuine preoccupation of a minority; the *Gymnasium* was of necessity therefore an institution for the education of a cultivated élite.

The rejuvenation of the *Gymnasium* in Humboldt's time gave it a status that it has retained ever since. But in inspiration it perhaps inevitably fell short of what its architect had envisaged. The demand that pupils should become at home in all branches of knowledge came to be more significant than the requirement that they should be fired by a spontaneous enthusiasm for the process. It is commonly alleged that the growth in importance of the school-leaving examination, the *Abitur,* caused more and more emphasis to be placed on sheer accumulation of knowledge in order to satisfy examiners to the detriment of the spirit of scholarly endeavour. It certainly would appear that in the course of the nineteenth century the process of *teaching* attracted much more interest than the process of *learning.* As new disciplines developed and secured their place in the school curriculum the increased demands of an encyclopedic approach put a premium on the skill of making the wealth of information digestible. The introduction of the name of Herbart in this connection would appear to cast him as the villain of the piece. This is neither just nor intended, for he has been as much the victim of misinterpretation as Humboldt. His work is relevant in that it epitomises an orderly approach to teaching which is of significant value as a framework but can all too easily become ossified as unimaginative routine.

HERBART AND THE FIVE STEPS

Johann Friedrich Herbart was born at Oldenburg in 1776, the son of a lawyer. After studying law himself at Jena, somewhat unenthusiastically, he spent two years as a private tutor in Switzerland in the course of which he added education to a range of interests that included above all philosophy. He then lectured in philosophy at Göttingen, becoming professor at Königsberg in succession to Kant. While in Switzerland he was able to visit Pestalozzi's school at Burgdorf and became preoccupied with the task of establishing the general principles that lay behind what he had observed, principles which he maintained could be applied at all levels of education. He explored the problem of arousing interest in the learner, attempting to determine why one experience rather than another should engage the attention. His analysis of the process led to a classification on which he based the universal method for which he is primarily remembered. This method has since been specifically categorised as the "five formal steps" of preparation, presentation, association, generalisation, and application, the whole constituting a doctrine of orderly presentation of new experience. The accuracy of Herbart's analysis of the process of thought was so convincing that it was widely adopted as the definitive method of instruction in all spheres. The exaggerated formalism that characterised teaching in German schools as a result of this does less than justice to the work of such a remarkable pioneer of educational theory. Herbart's method was no more than a guideline, and capable of varied elaboration. To treat it as dogma was mistaken but was a course easily followed in the nineteenth century when loyalty and obedience were high on the list of virtues to be fostered in schools. Formal expository methods helped to create the atmosphere of orderliness and discipline that was highly valued.

THE CATALOGUE OF CRITICISMS

By the early years of the twentieth century German schools were in the grip of an orthodoxy which attracted adverse comment on a number of counts. Some of these criticisms have been alluded to already, and it is perhaps appropriate now to summarise them in order better to understand the reactions which led to the growth of a radical movement.

Firstly, there was the quantity of information to be absorbed. In the secondary sphere the primary position of the classics in the curriculum had been challenged by the increasing interest in the newer disciplines of modern languages and natural science. These latter subjects were the specialisms of new modern schools which, as their name of *Realschulen* indicates, aimed to give a more realistic and relevant education. The *Gymnasien*, concerned to preserve their monopoly of preparation for university entrance, responded to the challenge by broadening their curriculum to take account of new interests. But the classics retained a large share of the time allocation, for it is generally easier to add to a curriculum than to reduce it. Consequently there were complaints of over-burdening of the pupils who were the victims of this struggle to preserve prestige. Not surprisingly it was a prestige that rankled with the *Realschulen* which aspired to the coveted name of *Gymnasium*. To achieve it, some of them began to build up their teaching of Latin so that in this sector too the demands on pupils became increasingly heavy. Finally, all of this in turn affected the elementary schools which tended to anticipate the pursuit of encyclopedic knowledge of the secondary stage.

The second major criticism concerned internal organisation. Each class was treated as a unit and the pupils in it were intended to stay together for all subjects throughout their school career. Specific standards had to be reached by the end of each year, and since there was so much ground to be covered a good deal of effort had to go into ensuring that all members of the class reached these. Those who failed to do so, even in one or two subjects, were made to repeat the year's work, the practice known as *sitzen bleiben*. This inflexible procedure had an element of mass pro-duction about it, with no allowance made for the unorthodox, for unusual strengths and weaknesses. Small wonder that under these conditions the standard method developed by Herbart seemed so apposite and, indeed, the third criticism levelled at the schools was the excessive formalism of the methods used. Whatever the expository expertise of the teacher, his pupils were expected at all times to absorb passively the material that was placed before them. Rigidity begets rigidity, and this formalism in turn went hand in hand with a fourth characteristic, namely an inflexible discipline which required unquestioning obedience, and thereby tending to exclude spontaneous inquiry. Punishments were alleged to be frequent and unconstructive. Finally, it is clear that an education composed of the foregoing catalogue of rigidities must to some extent stifle independent thinking. The authoritarian schools both reflected and supported a society in which obedience and industriousness were more highly valued than independence of mind and individual initiative. Furthermore, the prevailing canon of social behaviour in schools was conducive to the survival of a hierarchical structure in society as a whole.

One last point should be emphasised with regard to the nineteenth-century tradition, namely the social exclusiveness that it encouraged. Humboldt had envisaged the *Gymnasium* as a community of able scholars enthusiastically pursuing the high culture conveyed by the concept of *Bildung*. But it became the institution which ensured access to the leading positions in society. Consequently it was patronised predominantly by the middle class and a number of factors, in particular its intimidating scholarly aura and the requirement to pay fees and forgo earnings, discouraged the working class from entertaining any thought of sending children to it. The age of entry from the elementary school was 9 and, furthermore, in many cases early education was in private preparatory schools so that the sphere of academic education stood some way apart from the elementary education provided for the great majority of the population.

Not only was there a dualism based on class and insufficiently related to ability where the *Gymnasium* sector was concerned, it was in addition ineffective as regards the needs of the majority who attended the *Volksschule*, followed perhaps by some kind of further education in evening classes during the period of apprenticeship. For this sector was very much in the shadow of the dominant ideal of general education and made little provision for practical instruction geared to future vocational needs. Even the *Realschulen*, which set out to be more in tune with contemporary requirements, steadily edged towards the privileged position of the *Gymnasium*, and in so doing became preoccupied with orthodox academic aspirations. It was to the resulting lack of purpose in the education of the great majority of the population that Georg Kerschensteiner, one of the greatest figures in the radical tradition, was later to address himself.

EARLY RADICAL THOUGHT: FRIEDRICH FROEBEL

The origins of the radical tradition derive principally from Rousseau. In terms of individualistic practitioners seeking after new forms, his influence was particularly apparent in Germany and Switzerland. Ironically the same Pestalozzi whose school at Burgdorf inspired Herbart was also the inspiration for those innovators who sought to develop a view of education that was the antithesis of the somewhat inflexible regimentation of the orthodox German schools.

The most ardent of Pestalozzi's followers in Germany was Friedrich Froebel. He was born in 1782 in the village of Oberweissbach in Thuringia, the son of a pastor. His early education was no more than rudimentary, consisting of attendance at village schools followed by two years as an apprentice forester. At 17 he went to the university of Jena, an outsider as regards student life and ill equipped for studies which in any case he could not afford to complete. But the experience was sufficient to kindle his interest in philosophy, botany and zoology. After this abortive skirmish with the university world followed by some casual employment, he began teaching, first in Frankfurt and then at Pestalozzi's school at Yverdon. Here he was both inspired by the example of the master and motivated to advance his ideas a stage further. Of that time he wrote in his autobiography:

"The powerful indefinable stirring and uplifting effect produced by Pestalozzi set one's soul on fire for a higher, nobler life although he had not made clear or sure the exact way towards it nor indicated the means whereby to attain it. . . . I could see something higher and I believed in a higher efficiency, a closer unity of the whole educational system; in truth I believed I saw this clearer, though not with greater conviction than Pestalozzi himself."[1]

If he was now convinced that teaching was to be his vocation he was none the less aware of the deficiences of his own education, and he returned to his university studies, first in Göttingen then in Berlin where, after taking an interest in the whole gamut of scientific disciplines, he eventually specialised in mineralogy with such success that a distinguished academic career lay before him. However, nationalistic feeling impelled him to join the army and he served till the end of the war with France. It was then that he determined to devote his life to teaching. In 1816 he gathered together sufficient children to found a boarding school in Thuringia,

---

[1] *Autobiography of Friedrich Froebel,* translated by E. Michaelis and H. K. Moore, London, 1886, p. 79.

initially in Griessheim and moving in the following year to Keilhau. There he remained for fourteen years during which time he worked out his educational ideas and published them in a book called *The Education of Man (Menschenerziehung)*. When he left Keilhau it was to work in teacher training in Switzerland, and after a few years he was engaged in building up a model school at Burgdorf where Pestalozzi had worked before him. From then on he became more and more interested in the education of very young children. In 1840 he opened the first *Kindergarten* and for a decade he worked to propagate the ideas on which it was based. By 1850 many kindergartens had been established, but the movement was gathering momentum at an unpropitious time in German history. Unorthodox views of the kind held by Froebel and his associates were strongly disapproved of by the reactionary Prussian administration that followed the liberal revolt of 1848. The kindergarten was banned in 1851 and Froebel died in the following year.

If the orthodox school system forced a largely passive role on school pupils, the essence of Froebel's education lay at the opposite pole – activity. At Keilhau the pupils learnt by working together in a natural environment. The famous analogy which compared the child to a plant conveys the idea that education is a process of natural growth which can be guided but should not be forced. The task of the teacher was therefore to engineer situations in which natural learning could take place. Such situations must enable the child to satisfy the natural inner impulses to widen its experience through contact with nature and with other children and adults. For Froebel they took a multitude of forms, but whether it was reading or gardening, boatbuilding or acting, calculating or painting, every pursuit was intended to be characterised by spontaneous activity on the part of the pupils, calling whenever possible on a variety of aptitudes both intellectual and practical. It is not difficult to see how this view of education led Froebel in his later years to a consuming interest in the role of play in the education of very young children.

Froebel was well aware that individualistic, creative self-expression of this kind needed to be reconciled with the constraints of communal life. At Keilhau he was attempting to create a community which would develop in parallel with the development of its individual members through the experience of co-operative activity and service. It followed that there was no authoritarian hierarchy but a situation in which all members could learn to contribute to a commonly agreed view of how the community should be ordered. This is a further respect in which Froebel's ideas stood at an opposite pole to conventional practice in German schools of the nineteenth century. He was a pioneer of pupil participation in school government at a time when, as noted earlier, the prevailing ethos was sternly authoritarian. Froebel exerted a strong influence on future generations, notably on John Dewey in the United States, but he made little immediate impression on German education which continued to develop along the authoritarian lines already described and which eventually provoked the *Reform* movement which flowered in the early twentieth century. Then his themes of self-expression and self-government were taken up with renewed vigour.

REFORM THROUGH THE TEACHING OF ART

One of the first salvoes in this attack on the educational establishment was the publication in 1890 of a book entitled *Rembrandt as Educator,* anonymously ascribed to "a German" and which enjoyed a phenomenal success. The author, Julius Langbehn, declared that Germany stood on the threshold of a new era but could meet the challenge only by fulfilling the artistic potential of the nation. He attributed the encyclopedic culture of the *Gymnasium* to irrelevant foreign influences and called for a new individualism to be fostered through art teaching. Much of the appeal of Langbehn's writing undoubtedly lay in its nationalistic implications. It struck the same irrational chord as other outspoken critics of conventional culture such as Nietzsche. A series of art-teaching conferences later provided the forum for the exchange of ideas and thereby launched the new campaign for individualistic "child-centred" education.

A leading figure in the revival of art education was Alfred Lichtwark, a former elementary school teacher who had then become director of the Hamburg art gallery. His emphasis on the stimulation of the artistic sense epitomises a more general protest against traditional schooling. Drawing had been a part of the curriculum but had reached the stage where orderly presentation was more highly valued than evidence of artistic skill or originality. The view of Lichtwark and the others who met at the first Art Teaching Conference in Dresden in 1901 was that "we do not conceive of it [drawing] as a means to training in order, neatness, and mechanical accuracy as heretofore, but as the development of powers of comprehension and expression".[2] Two further conferences, at Weimar in 1903 and Hamburg in 1905, dealt with language and literature and with music and physical education respectively. On both occasions there were repeated declarations of the need for a free and creative atmosphere in the schools.

KERSCHENSTEINER AND VOCATIONAL EDUCATION

Another strand in the radical tradition, and the one which perhaps made the most lasting impression, is represented by the work of Georg Kerschensteiner who was born into an impoverished family in Munich in 1854. He began his career as an elementary teacher first in a small Bavarian village and later in Augsburg. Little over two years after taking up his first post, he gave up teaching in order to acquire a *Gymnasium* education, and at the age of 23 obtained the *Abitur*. He was now qualified to study at the university of Munich where six years later he was awarded a doctorate. At this point he returned to teaching, holding a succession of posts at *Gymnasien* in Nuremberg, Schweinfurt, and Munich, interspersed with a spell at the commercial school in Nuremberg. By the age of 40 he had made sufficient impact to be appointed Director of Education for Munich, a post that gave him the opportunity to put his ideas into practice. He built up a school system that left its mark on education throughout Germany.

Kerschensteiner was a man of wide interests. His doctorate had been for work on theories of electricity, but he taught mathematics to begin with and later developed a consuming interest in the teaching of nature study. He found art and music absorbing, too, and was an enthusiastic participant in intellectual life generally. By all accounts he was an accomplished teacher, both industrious and imaginative. Finding it irksome to confine his activities within the walls of the class room, he was a pioneer of field work in nature study, and he joined with his pupils in the pursuit of a variety of other extra-curricular activities. He saw the school as a community and education as a response to the needs of the individual child within it. These two insights, both originating in concern for the welfare of others, lay at the basis of his ideas and his activities as an education administrator in Munich.

[2] T. Alexander and B. Parker, *The New Education in the German Republic*, New York, 1929, p. 103.

They were insights which had much in common with the ideas of Froebel, but where these had in large measure implied exuberant recreation as the most educative activity, Kerschensteiner was much more concerned to stimulate learning through disciplined work. What he did share with Froebel and other radical thinkers was their opposition to a system that allotted a purely passive role to the pupil: for him the importance of activity was paramount. Indeed, the new genre which he created, the *Arbeitsschule,* though literally signifying "school for work", is generally translated as "activity school". What Kerschensteiner meant by activity was a combination of intellectual and practical pursuits. *Buchschule* (book school) was his disparaging term for the traditional type which was concerned exclusively with intellectual attainments and which in his view denied the child the opportunity to combine various aptitudes in order to conceive and produce a finished article. He saw practical activity of this kind as a fundamental psychological need of young people and was determined that it should be a standard component of the elementary curriculum.

The psychological argument in favour of a greater concern for practical work in schools was reinforced by utilitarian considerations. The great majority of elementary schoolchildren were destined to earn their living in manual work of one sort or another, and in Kerschensteiner's view were not well served by an education which was a pale shadow of the intellectual fare provided by the *Gymnasium* in the pursuit of general culture. Education had to be regarded as a preparation for life, and its content should therefore have some direct relevance to the way it would be lived. Here Kerschensteiner's work in further education was still more significant. The late nineteenth century had seen a good deal of interest in post-elementary education for the great majority outside the *Gymnasium* and *Realschule* and many continuation schools (*Fortbildungsschulen*) were established and flourished. They were bound by close organisational ties to the elementary schools, the six to eight weekly hours of instruction generally being given on the same premises in the evenings, and often by the same teachers. The curriculum, too, was along the same general lines as that of the elementary school. It was Kerschensteiner's achievement to transform this sector by creating schools in which the instruction was designed to be directly complementary to the learning of a trade through apprenticeship. This was the foundation of the *Berufsschule* system which has since played such a significant role in furnishing Germany with a well-trained skilled labour force. Kerschensteiner placed the individual trades at the centre of the instruction and forged links between the schools and the corresponding trade organisations. The co-operative spirit thrived, and in the decade before the First World War the system gathered such momentum that it was able to display undiminished vitality after Kerschensteiner's retirement from his directorship in 1919.[3]

The wider implications of Kerschensteiner's ideas on vocational education were that the process of learning to work efficiently was at the same time a valuable training in citizenship. A constant theme of his writings was that schools had in the past abdicated their responsibility to foster social virtues. To the degree that these had been developed, it was the family that had been responsible and, indeed, Kerschensteiner ascribed great importance to its role. His further education for girls was designed to equip them to be wives and mothers capable of running a home efficiently. But, in contrast to the family, "our schools make no systematic provision for fostering the higher social virtues – above all that sense of duty to the community which is of such immense importance, and the feeling of responsibility for every word and every act, the terrible lack of which brings about so much misfortune among our fellow-citizens".[4] Kerschensteiner wanted his schools to remedy this deficiency so that there would be developed in the masses what he called "a definite force in the cause of progress". This positive attitude to society he hoped would be engendered in schools which were concerned not so much with imparting to all their charges an all-round culture but rather with identifying specific aptitudes, mental and manual, and encouraging their development through diligent work.

With respect to the synthesis of the theoretical and the practical, Kerschensteiner shared a basic premise with the theorists of polytechnical education in the Soviet Union after the Revolution. His ideas had much to offer in the post-war period in the context of East German efforts to transform the traditional system. But he incurred the odium of socialists for his acceptance of the established order of society. Whatever the value

[3] For a full account of Kerschensteiner's life and work see Diane Simons, *Georg Kerschensteiner,* London, 1966.
[4] G. Kerschensteiner, *The Schools and the Nation,* translated by C. K. Ogden, London, 1914, pp. 12–13.

of his theories as regards educational psychology, politically speaking they were anathema. For example, he could write that "every step, even the smallest, in the direction which I have indicated will always bring a group of men nearer together than before: will teach them to serve, help, make sacrifices, and how to transform 'equality' into the acceptance of higher and lower in social organisation, and thousands of steps will do the same for a thousand groups".[5] It is scarcely surprising that a regime dedicated to the creation of a new social order denounced him. In a purely Western context the shortcomings of Kerschensteiner's ideas on civic education lay in their failure to develop critical faculties and independence of mind — qualities crucial to the survival of Weimar democracy.

Kerschensteiner made no arrogant claim that his contribution to educational theory and practice would be a panacea for this problem. He hoped it would achieve something, but his early diagnosis of the lack of civic virtues in German society was proved sadly accurate. Such civic education as there was was the work of the family. This is the point also made much later by Ralf Dahrendorf, namely that "the German school fails to render even what little contribution is left to it to strengthening of public virtues; it remains within the dominant world of the private values of the family".[6] For, in fact, in the 1950s it was evident from the course of social and, more specifically, educational policy that there was in the Federal Republic widespread acceptance of the importance of the family and the need to preserve its autonomous rights. This survival of faith in the values of the family in fact represents a failure on the part of the National Socialist regime to erode them for, to quote Dahrendorf once again:

"National Socialist school policies, and even more strongly the significance of obligatory membership in the Hitler Youth for all children from ten years of age, involved an increasing and deliberate restriction of familial rights and tasks. The Hitler Youth emphasized even among the ten-year-olds independence from, and indeed — exploiting the age-old antagonism of generations — hostility towards their parents. Total power involves at least the intention of permanent

5 G. Kerschensteiner, *op. cit.*, p. 25.
6 R. Dahrendorf, *Society and Democracy in Germany*, London, 1968, pp. 317-18.

control of every person by the rulers and their organizations. Such control presupposes the extrication of people from all social spheres that are removed from the grasp of public agencies. In this sense, the family was an obstacle on the path to the establishment of total power. In this sense the educational policies of the Nazis promoted public values — if in the form of the public vices of uniformed demonstrations, the denunciation of friends, and unquestioned activities of other kinds."[7]

While the reassertion of familial rights should be seen in the light of a reinstatement of humane values it must also be pointed out that for many of those preoccupied with the issue of social change it has appeared to constitute an obstacle in the path of a transition from a hierarchical and authoritarian society to an egalitarian and democratic one. It is a common thesis that the former is reflected in the tripartite school system, and the requirement to defend the rights of parents in everything to do with the education of their children has in the post-war period been one of the bastions of this system. In order fully to appreciate why traditional values survived, however, it is necessary to return to an examination of the opposition to conventional education in the early part of this century.

THE YOUTH MOVEMENT AND THE PROGRESSIVE SCHOOLS

Some indication of the disenchantment with the conventional school system is given by the growth of a radical movement among young people. The *Wandervögel* — as they called themselves on account of the hiking (*Wandern*) which was the common activity that united them — were critical of the conventional code of loyalty, obedience, and service to the Reich. Their protest was a spontaneous affirmation of the value of individual freedom and the importance of personal happiness. The ideas lacked clarity and cohesion, for they embraced a variety of strands of thinking from romantic glorification of the Middle Ages to advocacy of practical reforms in the German society of the twentieth century. This variety was reflected in a range of individual factions that did not easily coexist. Yet for all the patchwork nature of the movement it is possible to discern general characteristics. The *Wandervögel* were positive and idealistic,

---

[7] *Ibid.*, pp. 410-11.

sincere in their search for a less regimented way of life in which individualism could flourish. They were for the most part nationalistic, though in the early days not many were narrowly so. They were drawn from the middle class, mainly *Gymnasium* pupils and university students. And while they formally disclaimed any interest in politics the great majority were specifically opposed to socialism or social democracy, and by this token were, in fact, adopting political stances that ranged from the centre to the right.

The movement began in 1901 and reached a climax at a famous open-air convention on the Hohe Meissner mountain near Kassel in 1913. Soon after this it was swamped by the wave of national sentiment that carried Germany through the early stages of the war. When peace was restored the ranks of the *Wandervögel* were decimated, for many had died and many more lost interest. Though the survivors regrouped and resumed their activities, the movement was more fragmented than before. It also became more overtly political, rivalling and eventually being forced to capitulate to the Hitler Youth. In the present context it is interesting to note that in the earlier days of the Youth Movement major figures in education were significant influences. Langbehn's *Rembrandt as Educator,* for example, was widely read, and one of the most charismatic leaders, Gustav von Wyneken, was co-founder with Paul Geheeb of the famous progressive school at Wickersdorf. These two men derived their original momentum in this direction from their association with Hermann Lietz, perhaps the earliest significant protagonist of progressive schools. Lietz influenced a number of other leading figures in independent education, including Kurt Hahn, headmaster of Salem on Lake Constance and subsequently of Gordonstoun in Scotland. Indeed, it would be tempting to talk of a progressive school movement with common objectives were it not that, firstly, there was no cohesive group involved, and, secondly, that among those who did collaborate the many quarrels only confirmed that the common denominators were resolute individualism and force of character. A brief survey of their work, however, helps to highlight the characteristics of the State system against which they were reacting.

A useful starting point is the contrast drawn by Sir Michael Sadler in his Report to Parliament of 1898 entitled *Problems in Prussian Secondary Education for Boys, with special reference to similar questions in England.* He contrasts the "robust individualism" fostered in English schools with "the collective effort of a disciplined multitude" which he found in the German system:

> "Those who profit most by the freedom of the more individualising system often retain a greater keenness and freshness of mind, and therefore avail themselves more fully of later opportunities of self-improvement. In the second place, it is necessary to determine which effect on the whole is the better — the securing of a high level of average quality with some depression of the stronger individualities, or a great diversity of attainment and aptitude ranging from the very highest excellence to extreme dulness and ignorance. Here the German system seems to tend on the whole to produce the first result; the English system the second. But it is in the nature of the case that the English system of schools cannot present the particular kinds of excellence of organisation which will be expected in the German. National energy and thought have been poured, for a much longer time and with much greater intensity of effort, into their educational system than into ours."[8]

In this assessment Sadler saw the merits of the German secondary schools, their high standards of organisation and scholarship, the clarity of their objectives, and he acknowledged the achievement of the State authorities in building up such an efficient system. But he went on to emphasise the high degree of State control of education which had developed during the nineteenth century, well in excess of what Humboldt had originally envisaged, and to point out that the characteristic English reaction was to resist such control: "those who were naturally the keenest advocates of higher [in this context, secondary] education were at the same time the least anxious that it should be brought in any way under State control".[9]

In the light of this comment it comes as no surprise that Lietz gained the inspiration for his experiment during a period spent teaching in England at the progressive school of Abbotsholme. As a testament to the value of this experience he wrote *Emlohstobba* (the name of the school spelt backwards) and in 1898 he opened the first of a group of schools which he called *Deutsche Landerziehungsheime*. The overriding aim of a

---

[8] Education Department, *Special Reports on Educational Subjects*, Vol. 3, HMSO, London, 1898, p. 89.

[9] *Ibid.*, p. 96.

Landerziehungsheim was to create an autonomous community life which Lietz believed to be the essential medium for education. Such a view ran counter to the traditional German glorification of the importance of family life alluded to earlier. The communal life which Lietz built up embraced a strong emphasis on the appreciation of nature – in a way reminiscent of Froebel. There was, too, an affinity with the Youth Movement, for the enthusiasm for the outdoor life implied a reaction against the excessively intellectual diet of the State schools. To modern ears the heartiness and wholesomeness carry more than a hint of caricature:

> "The day begins early. Before six o'clock in summer the boys spring out of bed, dress lightly, and are off for a run in the morning air. With a teacher beside them they race across the meadows and through a forest path that brings them back to the school. They are under the showers and into their clothes in a few minutes. Most of them wear sandals, short trousers so that their knees are bare, and soft collars open at the throat. For sports and work in the fields they often strip to the waist so that their bodies are browned by the sun. Neither style nor care for their clothes checks them in vigorous activities, and the boys give an impression of freshness and fitness."[10]

Yet at the same time this account by a contemporary American observer conveys the drive and zest that their creator was able to infuse into the schools. Though there are parallels with English boarding schools, the Lietz schools were much smaller, the first three to be founded together numbering at most 300 pupils. These were grouped in a three-tier system: Ilsenburg for those aged 6–10, Haubinda for the 11–14-year-olds, and Bieberstein for the 15–18 age group. In his later years Lietz became a prey to xenophobia, and is accused of having associated himself strongly with the reactionary forces that had led Germany into the 1914-18 war.[11] After his death in 1919 the schools continued, seven in number, and eventually came to be run by Nazi sympathisers.

Among those who followed in the wake of Lietz, two have already been mentioned, Wyneken and Geheeb. After they had built up the Free School

[10] Alexander and Parker, *op. cit.*, p. 185.
[11] Minna Specht and Alfons Rosenberg, *Experimental Schools in Germany*, German Educational Reconstruction pamphlet, No. 1, London, 1946, p. 6.

Community (*Frei Schulgemeinde*) at Wickersdorf, Geheeb broke away to set up the Odenwald School near Heidelberg. Both men differed in outlook from Lietz. Wyneken's approach was much less emotional; his rationality led him, for example, to oppose the dominance of the classics in the curriculum and he was much less nationalistic. He found Lietz's system somewhat primitive but he did share with him the concern to build up a community that fostered the full range of activities. This was true, too, of Geheeb at the Odenwald school. In his case the divergence from the principles on which Lietz worked lay in his vigorous championship of individual development. The *Landerziehungsheime* had had a certain collectivism about them, coloured by a nationalism which demanded that their pupils give themselves to the "service of the German people". Geheeb worked on a principle of self-determination and wished to respect and promote what he called the "infinite variety of unique individuals".[12]

To the famous institutions built up by these three men should be added, among others, the name of Salem, founded in 1919 by Prince Max of Baden. His aim was to preserve something of the values which he saw being eroded at a time of instability; to counteract what he called "that self-satisfied individualism which nursed itself at the expense of community, criticising without the will to help. . . Plato's demand is as valid as ever: 'He who wishes to help his people must combine the power to think with the power to act'."[13]

The initiative of Prince Max needs to be seen in the context of the period of demoralisation after the First World War; it was his hope that Salem would lead the way in reviving German national feeling. For its headmaster Kurt Hahn, the most important feature of the school was that it was a community attempting to draw on the best of earlier experience in this kind of education and develop in its pupils self-reliance and a sense of service. For his opposition to Hitler, Hahn was imprisoned and then forced into an exile which led him to found Gordonstoun where his ideals of service could be pursued further. Also founded in 1919 was the first of the Rudolf Steiner schools which have continued to thrive up to the present day; these are dealt with at greater length in Chapter 5.

Though by virtue of their pioneering work the boarding schools occupy a unique place in the development of German education, they made as a

[12] *Ibid.*, p. 10.
[13] Wend Graf Kalnein, *Salem,* Lindau and Constance, 1958, p. 34.

group relatively small inroads into the State system. Their orthodoxy appealed to only a small section of the middle class. It was no doubt within the means of many more to patronise them but, unlike their counterparts in England who opted for the public schools, on the whole they disapproved of boarding. This was an attitude that Wyneken in particular inveighed against in his writings. How many parents, he asked, had taken the trouble to think seriously about education and how many lacked the natural ability to understand children, a capacity by no means guaranteed to accompany the ability to produce them? But such arguments had little effect, and the fact that some of the schools pioneered co-education made the middle class regard them with still greater suspicion. In the last analysis it was always the *Gymnasium* with its stern disciplines which was considered to provide the most appropriate education. In a word it represented the establishment.

GYMNASIUM AND *EINHEITSSCHULE*

For this it came under fire from another quarter. To be sure the *Gymnasium* was part of the State system and accessible to many more than just the sons and daughters of those who could afford the fees of the private schools. But in left-wing circles the State system itself was seen as a bastion of privilege, with the *Gymnasium* catering overwhelmingly for the middle class and the *Volksschule* for the great majority of the population. During the period of the Weimar Republic there were many calls for the creation of an *Einheitsschule,* the term used to denote a totally re-organised system along what would today be called comprehensive lines, providing equal opportunity for all young people on the basis of merit and without regard to social origin. There were, too, practical experiments to see how schools would function under such conditions. It was not merely a matter of structures; various curricular implications were involved. While some of the established *Gymnasium* teachers might well have favoured equality of opportunity they showed solidarity in their defence of the high culture based on rigorous study of classical and modern languages and literature. Only within the context of the preservation of this culture undiluted were they prepared to support efforts to encourage a higher representation from the working class in their schools. Thus it was on curricular grounds that they defended the existing system. The 1920s saw a vigorous continuing debate between this faction and the radicals who were concerned to pioneer new structures.

The more revolutionary end of the radical spectrum is represented by Paul Oestreich, the Berlin teacher who in 1919 founded the League of Radical School Reformers (*Bund entschiedener Schulreformer*). This group, with which were associated the names of many prominent personalities with strong left-wing views – among others Fritz Karsen, Siegfried Kawerau, Anna Siemsen, and Elisabeth Rotten – was not prepared to operate in the so-called "educational province" which was traditionally regarded as lying outside the domain of politics. They were critical in general of the anodyne social democracy of Weimar which they saw as failing to meet the needs of society, and in particular of the failure to use the school system to promote the development of "the free people's State and the spirit of a social community that embraces the whole of mankind". The first specific proposal of the League was to overcome institutional differentiation by means of an "elastic" *Einheitsschule,* consisting of a four-year primary, a five-year lower secondary, and a three-year upper secondary stage. The middle stage was to have three broad streams with provision for the beginnings of such a division in the last two primary years. The curriculum was to be organised on a "core and course" basis, i.e. with a compulsory minimum and a variety of options to be chosen according to inclination and ability. A subsequent revision of this plan laid less stress on internal differentiation while more specifically socialist demands such as secularity and whole day attendance came to the fore.

To some extent Oestreich and his associates were in sympathy with the main stream of the *Reform* movement. They put forward the notion that the school should cease to present a catalogue of knowledge and skills that was regarded as the sum of a national culture, and to which pupils had to adapt; rather it behoved the *schools* to do the adapting that would enable them to meet the needs of the individual child. Additionally, however, the left-wing radicals saw such individual needs within the context of society in general, and a different kind of society at that. The political implications of their view that social conditions must be changed can more clearly be seen in an extension of the *Einheitsschule* idea, put forward originally by the Russian educationist Blonski, and taken up in Germany by such people as Siegfried Kawerau and Anna Siemsen. This was the *Produktionsschule,* a concept that involved the incorporation of the school into industry. School would no longer be, as it were, one of the luxury goods of capitalist society to be enjoyed to the full by a small minority; rather would all children derive from their school experience practical understanding of the means of production and, by implication, the foundations would be laid for collective control of these means. As it happened, factory-based instruction remained a theoretical concept, and the experiments that were carried out generally took the form of school farms. Moreover, in the present-day *DDR*, where polytechnical education involves close links between schools and factories, this early pioneer work meets in retrospect with no less derision than that with which the efforts of the *Reform* movement as a whole are viewed. Apart from Oestreich himself, who enjoyed the respect of East German educationists both before and after his death in 1959, the men and women who formed the League of Radical School Reformers are held to have compromised with capitalist society and thereby to have failed to promote a revolutionary new order.

A number of other prominent figures should be mentioned in the context of the *Einheitsschule* experiments. Fritz Karsen was particularly concerned with the problem of bringing about a rapprochement between school and "life" but recognised that the idea of an individual production school was unacceptable since it did not furnish an appropriate environment for children; his view was that the demands of an authentic production situation necessitated constraints that would inhibit their powers. Instead he coined the term *Erlebnisschule* – "experience school" – and in the school complex which he ran in the Neukölln district of Berlin a whole catalogue of experimental ideas were tried out between 1921 and 1933:

"Those who collaborated with Karsen in those years will never be able to forget how, brick by brick, the new school organisation became a reality. It began with the creation of a new *Aufbauschule*. In contrast to its counterparts that already existed in such areas, this new city school was dedicated to the task of identifying and cultivating gifted children from the working class. New teaching methods were introduced (withdrawal of the teachers to some extent into the background, quadrangular seating of classes, presentation of subject-matter by individual pupils, keeping of records – minutes, as it were – of class activity, discussion of schedules of work); all school punishments were suspended; the marks traditionally given were partially replaced by verbal reports on work or extensive assessments of a more general kind; visits to factories and firms were arranged, as were study tours of various kinds; specialist subject rooms on the American model were provided and block timetabling so organised that there was always a change of room after a double period of instruction; a comprehensive school library was built up; amateur dramatics were encouraged; there were reports on pupils' work and exhibitions of it at the end of the school year; the school was co-educational; study seminars were set up for the training of teachers."[14]

The atmosphere established in the *Aufbauschule* then gradually came to permeate the entire complex of schools under Karsen's aegis, extending most notably into the area of further education whereby young workers were enabled and encouraged to work for the *Abitur* and thereby qualify themselves for university.

Another important figure was Peter Petersen, the Jena professor of education who under the auspices of the university built up a school in which experiments could be systematically monitored. Petersen aimed above all at flexibility, breaking down the rigid system whereby the pupils of each class stayed together for all subjects throughout their school career and those who failed to reach the required standard in individual subjects were refused promotion and made to repeat the year's work. He was also opposed to arbitrary boundaries between subjects and was a pioneer investigator of the process of learning through group activity. The "Jena Plan", first put forward in 1919, reflected his concern to promote equality of opportunity which he interpreted in a meritocratic sense, guaranteeing the promotion of the interests of the more able within the comprehensive framework. This plan, famous throughout Germany, was particularly influential in the state of Thuringia where a comprehensive school system was operated in the period from 1922 to 1924.

The interests of the teachers as a whole, particularly those in the *Volksschule*, were represented by the general secretary of the German Teachers Union (*Deutscher Lehrerverein*), Johannes Tews. He, too, presented a plan for an *Einheitsschule* structure based on a six-year primary school and fully articulated up to university level. All of these

---

[14] T. Wilhelm, *Pädagogik der Gegenwart,* Stuttgart, 1967, p. 93.

ideas and many others were ventilated at length at the massive Reich conference of all those with a stake in the future of German education. The variety of interests represented and of views put forward is indicated by the fact that there were some 700 participants. And there was a corresponding variety of tensions inhibiting collaboration between *Reich* and *Länder* in defining the national education policy. These tensions — e.g. socialist versus Christian objectives or Bavaria versus The Rest — in general matters of policy led to the anti-climactic outcome that the only kind of agreement that could emerge was mandarin-style documentation of contemporary trends in educational thought. A unifying theme remained beyond reach.

The desire to find such a unifying theme had become increasingly explicit during the years that led up to the First World War. It had been a major worry of the Weimar Conference of 1903 that the low prestige enjoyed in intellectual circles by everything German was stifling appreciation of autochthonous language, literature, and art. This kind of discussion betrayed a feeling that the idealism of the Humboldt era had faded away and been replaced by the pursuit of individual specialisms lacking a common denominator: the ideal of the rounded personality steeped in the culture of antiquity had, it seemed, given way to the reality of the expert concerned only with his own narrow field. Hans Breuer, in the foreword to the 1913 edition of the *Zupfgeigenhansl,* the song book of the Youth Movement, wrote disparagingly of "the semi-existence of the specialist and the expert". It was one of the cherished ambitions of the movement to seek out a new version of the old ideal in the cultural roots of the German people. This tendency had been not inappropriate in the wartime period when urgent priority was given to the promotion of national unity and patriotism. The emphasis on specifically German culture is epitomised by the title of a book by Hugo Gaudig, *Deutsches Volk — Deutsche Schule (German People — German School)* which appeared in 1917.

Though the Reich Conference failed in the task of gathering up these threads into some kind of unified approach, an important development in this direction took place as a result of the efforts of Hans Richert, an official of the Prussian Ministry of Education, who was greatly exercised by this problem. His conception of unity lay in a new emphasis on those subjects that were, or could be made to be, concerned with specifically

German culture — the mother tongue, religious instruction, history, geography, and civics — and which were common to the curriculum of all types of school. By means of this core of *"Kulturkunde"* the German cultural heritage was to be absorbed and this was regarded as the fundamental task of the schools. It was pointed out with some force that schools were not preparatory institutions for specific professions or university faculties and that neither of these spheres was to influence what happened in them. The core curriculum was therefore not merely common to all types of school; it was to stand at the very centre of school activity in the belief that it would unify the system despite the other differences in curriculum as between the *Gymnasium*, the *Realgymnasium*, the *Oberrealschule*, and the newly created genre the *Deutsche Oberschule* of which German language and literature was the particular specialism.

The significance of Richert's contribution to the development of German education does not, however, lie in the innovation it brought, for the *Deutsche Oberschule* with its nationalistic flavour was seized upon by the Nazis as the model for the future. Richert is important rather for his work in clarifying and consolidating the position of what were to become the three major types of *Gymnasium*. These developed out of the distinction in Richert's time between the *Gymnasium*, the *Realgymnasium*, and the *Oberrealschule* — specialising in classics, modern languages, and mathematics/natural sciences respectively — and later became the basis for secondary education in the post-war system. For after 1945 it was to this *Gymnasium* tradition and to the tradition of a *Volksschule* strongly under Church influence that West Germans turned for inspiration in the urgent task of educational reconstruction. On the other hand, the pioneers of the *Einheitsschule* and their heirs made relatively little impact at a time when the mood of the country was predominantly conservative. The minority radical tradition found an outlet in the Soviet Zone during the early years of the Occupation; but as the school system developed further in the *DDR* it ceased to owe a great deal to pre-war German models.

CHAPTER 3

Economic Recovery and Social Development

The various explanations of the economic miracle indicate a post-war situation in which German industry was extraordinarily well placed to take advantage of world demand for manufactured goods. Generous funds were made available through Marshall Aid to finance the swift modernisation of plant that was necessary; the two sides of industry were united in their determination to make good the losses incurred in the war; the urge to rebuild for the long term was not accompanied by excessive expectations for the short term, consequently rises in incomes were moderate, savings and investment significant. The happy coincidence of factors such as these following in the wake of the currency reform of 1948 made possible a rapid rise to prosperity.

A good deal of the diagnosis of the favourable circumstances concerns the qualities of the German people. They are frequently described as industrious, methodical, single-minded, and whatever reservations may accompany generalisations of this kind, it is beyond doubt that industrial training was organised in such a way as to ensure the output of an efficient labour force. This success cannot be attributed primarily to the full-time compulsory education that was provided, for the great majority of children attended elementary school for eight years only, leaving at the age of 14. Much more significant was the provision for apprenticeship linked with part-time schooling to the age of 18 in a *Berufsschule*. The establishment of compulsory attendance of this kind had been an early achievement of the Weimar Republic. It complemented the instruction given to apprentices on the job, and together the two elements constituted the foundations of the impressive edifice of German technical education.

THE ROLE OF VOCATIONAL TRAINING

Perhaps the most striking feature was the convergence of interests concerned and the seriousness of purpose that arose out of this. Employers were legally obliged to co-operate in such matters as the release of employees for attendance at the *Berufsschule* and the provision of adequate instruction on their own premises. The larger enterprises were, naturally enough, better equipped for this, but the programmes of instruction were standardised nationally in that each trade had a "profile", known as the *Berufsbild*, representing an inventory of the knowledge and skills that it demanded. On this analytical basis it was possible to organise systematic schemes of work and to record progress methodically. Furthermore, the examinations and tests which apprentices had to undergo were conducted according to nationally agreed standards. Committees of examiners included representatives from management, from the staff of the *Berufsschulen*, and from those entrusted with the instruction given on the job, while the entire procedure took place under the eye of the Chambers of Industry and Commerce and of Crafts, the employers' associations, and the trade unions. All of this did much to ensure that the qualifications awarded carried a guarantee of competence and were valuable currency in the national labour market.

It was this value that constituted the attraction for the clientele of the system. The acquisition of a trade qualification was considered a sound investment which justified the postponement of earnings that had to accompany it. For apprentices were paid very little; in fact the money they did receive was technically regarded as a grant towards their maintenance while they completed their education. Herein lay the danger that they were being used as cheap labour. But charges of this kind were seldom levelled at employers during the rise to prosperity, such was the desire to acquire the security that went with possession of a certificate.

It fitted in very well with post-war economic policy that vocational training should be largely in the hands of industry and commerce and not directly the concern of the education ministries. The essence of the policy of the "social market economy" which was espoused after the war was that the responsibility of the government went no further than to create a framework within which entrepreneurial initiative could flourish and where, as a corollary, State intervention would be minimal. The

apprenticeship system existed first and foremost to serve private enterprise, allowing the employers to train young people in the way they
considered most appropriate, and it was generally assumed that the
interests of the trainees themselves would, equally, be well served by this
dispensation. While the potential conflict between the two sets of interests
can readily be seen, the system enjoyed widespread acceptance by virtue
of its ability to meet the relatively modest social and economic
expectations of the great majority of young people. Marxist interpretations of the situation did, it is true, emphasise the element of
exploitation of labour for capitalist gain, but the prevailing climate of
opinion was strongly anti-Communist, as the defeats suffered by the
SPD in the *Bundestag* elections of 1953 and 1957 showed. There is little
doubt that the absence of great dissatisfaction on social grounds with the
provision of education and training enhanced the prospects of economic
advance.

SOCIAL STRATIFICATION AND MOBILITY

In this serene picture there appeared very little obvious awareness of
the degree of social segregation that was reflected in the education system.
Such awareness as there was among the working class aroused little resentment at a time of bountiful employment prospects in industry and
commerce. When this is taken into account the contrast can be seen
between the vocational route with its tangible attractions, on the one
hand, and the rather more nebulous pursuit of general culture in the
academic *Gymnasium*, on the other. To follow the course to the school-
leaving certificate, the *Abitur*, in the latter required nine years and sometimes longer on account of the practice of repeating grades mentioned in
Chapter 1. When the examination was completed successfully, usually at
the age of 20 or so, it was normal to proceed to the university, for the
Gymnasium curriculum was conceived of as having primarily this kind of
propaedeutic function. Such a path was costly since school fees were
abolished only by degrees during the 1950s, and State financial support for
full-time students in higher education was rare. Under such conditions it is
obvious enough that the separate paths of general education and
vocational training strongly mirrored social differences. The *Gymnasium*
was the preserve of the middle class and was penetrated by only a small

proportion of working-class children. For the great majority of the latter an apprenticeship with a reputable firm was the natural aspiration. For those with higher ambitions, very often the intermediate *Realschule* was more attractive than the forbiddingly academic *Gymnasium*.

It is not true to say that no official interest was taken in the kind of segregation that operated within the education system. The Commission set up in 1953 known as the *Deutscher Ausschuss* issued a series of brief analyses and recommendations which reveal in particular a consciousness of the inadequacy of the elementary schools which provided the only full-time education available to the great majority. But though they reflected a growing concern among educationists the recommendations made little impact on the general public until the publication of an "outline plan" for development, the *Rahmenplan*, in 1959. The proposals which it contained and which are described in detail in the next chapter appear in retrospect remarkably anodyne. What is more there was no obligation on any of the *Länder* to adopt them, the function of the Commission being purely advisory. But though they constituted no very radical challenge to the existing order it is clear from the lively controversy that they stirred up that education had emerged as a sensitive issue. While reformist groups formulated plans for more thoroughgoing changes than those contemplated, conservative factions defended the existing arrangements.

One element in the conservative argument is particularly significant for social development, namely that the proponents of change had little evidence to offer in support of their allegations about the injustices of the traditional system as restored after the war. By 1959 fee-paying had been done away with and the champions of the *Gymnasium* could claim that with open competition for entry at the age of 10, opportunities were distributed on the sole basis of intellectual merit or promise and that no child needed to be disadvantaged on social grounds. In this kind of thesis it was possible to beg such obvious questions as the predictive accuracy of entrance examinations, variations in rates of intellectual development, influence of family background on attainment, largely because of the paucity or absence of empirical studies of such matters. Allegation could be met with counter-allegation, and the onus was clearly enough on the reformers to substantiate their case. This situation gave rise to an abundance of investigations which in aggregate transformed the state of knowledge about the relationship between education and the social structure in Germany.

The economic recovery of the 1950s had the effect of consolidating the trend of development towards the kind of social structure associated with advanced industrial nations. Already in 1939 the proportion of the population engaged in agriculture in Germany had been small, some 15 per cent or so of the work force, and by 1965 the figure for the Federal Republic had fallen to around 10 per cent. The corollary of this was clearly enough an increase in the proportion employed in industrial production, but a further, later, trend has been the growth in the numbers employed in the service industries. This change in the broad pattern of distribution of employment has brought about a greater complexity in the social structure than was previously evident. In the past a small élite group at the top of the social hierarchy contrasted with a large underprivileged group at the bottom, the two being separated by a small, middle category: in modern society the two top groups have been slightly enlarged, but much more significantly the lowest-placed group has become differentiated to a greater degree than before. Education has been an important factor in this process.

The group at the top of the hierarchy is identifiable as being drawn from the professions, the upper echelons of the civil service, and from among those occupying the most responsible positions in large industrial and commercial undertakings. Despite the disruption of the war years and the widespread feeling that 1945 was the "year zero", it displayed substantial continuity with the traditions of the pre-war middle class, and this was particularly evident in the education of its members. Only the *Gymnasium* curriculum led logically to university, and consequently it was entry to the *Gymnasium* that largely determined future career prospects. Not only did investigations establish a very marked middle-class bias in recruitment to these schools, but they also showed that those who did enter them from the working class were far less likely to survive to the end of the exacting course. Thus the positions enjoying the highest status and rewards, for many of which *Gymnasium* and university education were indispensable prerequisites, continued to be filled predominantly by the most highly placed social group. And since the size of this category did not greatly increase as a proportion of the total working population, it followed that access to it from lower starting points on the social scale was comparatively rare. Consequently the inevitable accusation was that the *Gymnasium* was operating as an instrument for the self-perpetuation of an established élite.

It was below the level of the topmost social group that the substantial mobility in German society was evident. With the growth of affluence the proportion of semi-skilled and unskilled labourers fell by the 1960s to at most 20 per cent of the labour force. The changing situation in which so many more of the population were acquiring more complex skills is mirrored by the resulting need to import unskilled labour from abroad. This influx of between one and two million *Gastarbeiter* ("guest workers") from such countries as Italy, Turkey, and Yugoslavia created its own educational problems. For the present, the point is that the main mobility took place above the dwindling semi-skilled and unskilled category, that is to say among clerical and skilled workers, more and more of whom acquired further specialist training leading to more responsible jobs in industry, among small independent entrepreneurs, and among those employed in the rapidly expanding service industries. The education that facilitated this advancement lay largely outside the *Gymnasium*. Indeed, it was a well-known phenomenon that among working-class people who were ambitious for their children the intermediate *Realschule* was generally more attractive than the more academic alternative. In addition, the vocational and technical education sector offered a wide range of opportunities for professional advancement. There is little doubt, too, that these areas threw up new élites which enjoyed comparable wealth, if not comparable status of the traditional kind, to that of the longer established highly placed groups. None the less, the sociological investigators of equality of opportunity generally took access to the *Gymnasium* and university as their criterion of success. In this context appeared the frequently quoted statistic that while manual workers accounted for some 57 per cent of the working population, the proportion of university students from such origins was 4 per cent in 1950 rising to 7·5 per cent in 1970.

Among the many factors that are more generally quoted to account for the disproportionately low enrolments at universities among lower income groups, mention should be made of two which have particular relevance to Germany. The first has to do with the relationship between the *Gymnasium* and the home. To reiterate the point made in Chapter 1, classes in German schools are, generally speaking, conducted in the mornings only, the afternoons being devoted to homework. Parents often supervise this, indeed are often expected to do so by teachers. Since this is a task more easily carried out by those who are familiar and in sympathy with the academic aims of the school, it comes more easily to those parents who themselves have had a *Gymnasium* education; children whose parents are either unfamiliar with or hostile to the entire process are at an obvious disadvantage. To offset this a number of reform proposals have included plans for the introduction of whole-day attendance at school. The second factor has been the paucity of financial support for students on the part of the State. In 1953 some 56 per cent of university students were financed entirely out of parental means; by 1966 this figure had scarcely changed, in fact it had shown a slight increase to 57 per cent. The remainder were in 1953 financed either by various kinds of loans, State or private, or by part-time employment which accounted for 28 per cent. The situation was different in the 1960s in that a scholarship scheme known as the "Honnef Model" was in operation; in 1966 some 14·5 per cent of students were financed in this way, so that the numbers financing themselves solely through part-time employment fell to just under 11 per cent of the total.[1] Thus the introduction of State subsidies for students had very little effect on the social composition of the university population.

NEW PATTERNS IN VOCATIONAL TRAINING

It has already been hinted that the success of technical education and vocational training, building on the foundations of the apprenticeship system, had the effect of siphoning off potential discontent over the social inequality in general education. But however marked this success was in the decade of the economic miracle, it later became clear that there was a disturbing lack of co-ordination between the training of apprentices and their employment. Surveys which showed that half of those who qualified were no longer practising the trade they had learnt reflected a growing dissatisfaction with their education and training among these young people. They were more conscious of being exploited as cheap labour than their predecessors had been and more critical of the quality of instruction given on the shop floor. Added to this was the deterioration of standards

[1] *Wirtschaft und Statistik* 5, 1971, p. 294.

in the *Berufsschulen*, where investigations revealed that almost 40 per cent of teaching posts were vacant.

However, reform was not so much a matter of improving the existing arrangements. Changing patterns in employment were beginning to dictate a reappraisal of the principles on which the system was built up. In the course of the 1960s increasing emphasis was laid on the importance of flexibility in the labour force. Changes in industrial technology meant that new skills needed to be acquired more frequently and it became a commonplace observation that few people could expect any longer to practise the same expertise unchanged throughout a lifetime. Consequently experience yielded in importance to education which alone could guarantee that mastery of general principles which it was declared would promote widespread adaptability to technological change. When the system of vocational and technical education was surveyed in the light of this type of argument, it was found wanting. For while it is true that it offered ample opportunities for advancement, these were from a narrow base. There were some 500 or so trades for which apprentices could train, each with its own specific *Berufsbild*. In a situation where versatility was becoming the dominant aim, such a degree of specialisation was unacceptable.

The response to this situation came initially from individual firms, led by the pioneer work of the Krupp company, in the form of systems of "training by stages" (*Stufenausbildung*). Broadly speaking the schemes involved three stages, progressing from the general to the specific. A brief description of the procedure adopted by the steel combine IG Metall will serve to illustrate the approach. The first stage provided an identical curriculum for all trainee entrants to the steel industry, involving a ten-month induction into the basic techniques and skills of metal processing. At the end of this period apprentices took an aptitude test to assist them in the choice from among five more specialised groups in which the second stage would be pursued. Each of these groups involved a broad training within the area concerned leading to a skilled worker qualification valid for what were formerly a number of separate trades. At the end of this stage, lasting about two years, it was possible on the basis of a further aptitude test to continue training to a third level, that of qualified specialist. The advantages of the three-stage system as enumerated at a trade union seminar sponsored by OECD can be quoted as a summary of the thinking behind the new trend in vocational training:[2]

"1. It gives every adolescent a chance to receive a training corresponding to his wishes and aptitudes. It therefore takes account of aptitude and the possibility of employment. Apprentices who might at first sight seem unsuitable are no longer automatically excluded from training but given a chance to prove themselves. So-called "late developers" are thus at a lesser disadvantage.

"2. Vocational training biased towards a particular trade will make a correct decision easier for the adolescent. The grouping of similar trades also makes the choice of a specific job easier. Aptitude tests and examinations before training can largely be dispensed with, since during the first stage there is ample opportunity for the apprentice to show what he can do.

"3. A broadly based training results in greater mobility later on. It therefore meets the requirements of adaptation and continual further training for the more gifted employees.

"4. Vocational training centres and firms can more easily be co-ordinated within a system of training by stages than could otherwise be possible in view of the great variety of individual vocations and vocational training schemes.

"5. The training system by stages is able to produce better results. A specific curriculum obliges the trainees to follow a systematic and methodical training and dispenses with any unnecessary chance work. Since adolescents are admitted to each stage only once they have proved their aptitudes, failure in a particular examination can be avoided. As no unsuitable candidates are accepted, training can proceed at a quicker pace.

"6. Present-day final apprenticeship examinations are nothing but a display of a set skill. With training by stages where aptitude for basic skills has to be proved in the very first stage and mastery of more complicated tasks in the second, there is an opportunity for more meaningful, objective, and functional tests.

[2] Georg Benz, 'The three-stage system', in OECD, *Education and Training for the Metal Worker of 1980* (Regional Trade Union Seminar), Paris, 1968, pp. 233–4.

"7. Each stage comes to a self-contained and definite end. This avoids the distinction made between vocational trainees and apprentices which has worked to the psychological detriment of the latter."

However well thought out and promising this new system of training was, its great disadvantage was that it depended on the initiative of individual firms, and only the large ones were in a position to operate it effectively. But these had always had the resources to provide training of a high standard. It was among the smaller companies that the difficulties lay and that the discontent was most evident. Thus the earlier doctrine according to which the State eschewed intervention in industrial training was called into question, and from the mid-sixties onwards there was increased pressure for new legislation which led eventually to the passing of the Vocational Education Law (*Berufsbildungsgesetz*) of 1969.

The new view being taken of technical and vocational education should be seen in the context of a more general shift in attitudes to economic policy. Shortages of manpower arising from unbalanced provision for training were only one of a number of factors which combined to create an uneasiness about the development of the economy. The longstanding determination to have no truck with anything that smacked of a centrally planned socialist system weakened, and from about 1963 onwards demands grew for the co-ordination of economic measures on a national level. Federal intervention was increasingly canvassed as a means of off-setting the inequalities brought about by the minimal restrictions on private enterprise combined with the devolution of authority to the *Länder*. As might be expected of a social democratic party, the *SPD* favoured greater central control and was in a position to exert more and more influence, first as a partner in the Grand Coalition with the con-servative parties, the *CDU* and *CSU* of 1966, and later as the senior partner in *SPD/FDP* governments from 1969 onwards.

THE CAMPAIGN FOR EXPANSION

This general context explains the timeliness of Georg Picht's outburst in the "German Educational Catastrophe". His diagnosis of the threat posed to the economy by the failure to develop the education system seemed plausible because two major sources of highly qualified manpower had dried up. Firstly, the men of the older generation which had not suffered such heavy losses in the war had reached retirement age. Secondly, the influx of refugees from the *DDR* had been cut off by the erection of the Berlin Wall in 1961. The one issue that could be relied upon to arouse political interest in education was the question of the supply of manpower to maintain economic development. Picht appeared therefore to have a particularly telling argument when he suggested that France would forge ahead economically by virtue of having adopted a planned development through which the numbers passing the *baccalauréat*, the equivalent of the German *Abitur*, would greatly expand while Germany would gradually decline in competitiveness. On this basis an eloquent case was built up for a greater degree of central planning. This was the climate in which the *Bildungsrat* was set up to promote and monitor the expansion of the education system. The emphasis that Picht laid on the *Abitur* placed this at the centre of the controversy. The social argument for expansion based on various analyses of the degree of selectivity in the school system buttressed the economic argument of the need for more highly qualified manpower, so that a rise in the output of *Abiturienten* rapidly became the sacred cow of policy.

In the new atmosphere of political awareness the relationship between education and social stratification became much more obvious than ever before. For one thing, more and more evidence was piled up to demonstrate the social exclusiveness of the *Gymnasium*. For another, greater attention was now paid to the forces that had worked in favour of the retention of the elementary schools. The ethos of the *Volksschule* was one of undemanding homeliness, especially in the rural areas where in many small schools there was only one teacher for all the age groups. Picht was scathing about the "passionate advocates who love to sketch a homely still life of the fatherly figure of the village schoolmaster with children crowding round him like a family", and pointed out that schools of this kind were in no position to provide the minimum requirement for agricultural workers, industrial workers, and craftsmen in the modern age, far less to make possible transfer to higher stages of education. His strictures were subsequently reinforced by research which showed that in 33 per cent of parishes in the Federal Republic virtually no children stayed in full-time education beyond the school-leaving age and that in a further 15 per cent of parishes less than 5 per cent did so.[3] Thus large discrepancies

[3] H. Peisert, *Soziale Lage und Bildungschancen in Deutschland*, Munich, 1967, p. 53.

in opportunity as between rural and urban areas were demonstrated to a meticulous degree of detail.

The failure to develop the *Volksschulen* was not entirely through default. They constituted the one sector of the system in which Church influence was strong. Many of them were denominational, and the best prospect of maintaining them as such lay in resistance to any suggestion of a totally reorganised State system which would involve amalgamation of small schools and increased transfer to secondary schools which were non-denominational. This resistance to social and economic development became a political issue. The churches which had enjoyed a powerful revival immediately after the war were accused now of having taken advantage of their influence to exert political pressure against change in the education system. Certainly those interest groups with a strong religious affiliation had been among the most vociferous opponents of the *Rahmenplan.*

By the late 1960s, however, the campaign for expansion had gained in momentum. Economic arguments had always been potentially strong and, as noted earlier, had largely militated against change during the rise to prosperity. Now they were beginning to work in the other direction. Social arguments for equalisation of opportunity were also meeting with a more favourable reception among a population in which the younger generation which had reached adulthood since the war had become the majority. Though no major structural reforms were introduced in the majority of *Länder,* the change in attitudes heralded a much greater interest in and demand for education throughout the community. The new problem was whether it would be appropriately distributed. The danger was that the concentration of the argument on the acquisition of the *Abitur* would draw more and more young people away from the vocational sector which was beginning to decline in attractiveness. This was clearly recognised by the *Bildungsrat* which therefore argued the need for intervention, pointing out that it could no longer be accepted that the vocational sector should be regarded as self-administered, largely controlled by employers in accordance with the interests of their companies. Instead, it declared, the same educational principles and policy considerations should apply to the general and vocational spheres alike. While the *Bildungsrat* worked to incorporate vocational paths into its overall plan for the future of the system, the *Bundestag* passed its vocational education law, the *Berufsbild-*

ungsgesetz of 1969. This set up a structure of committees which, it was
intended, would intervene to correct abuses of the apprenticeship system;
but it left unchanged the division which allowed for only 20 per cent of
apprentices' time to be devoted to full-time theoretical instruction. While
it sought to encourage the development of the "three-stage system" it had
no powers to extend its implementation. It was therefore less a long-term
measure than a beginning to the process whereby the State increasingly
took responsibility for the education of all young people up to the age of
18.

The great advantage that lay in directing efforts mainly towards the
vocational sector was that this strategy offered the best prospect of
harmonising social and economic objectives. If the promotion of greater
opportunity for advancement was concentrated in the field of general
education it would not necessarily be economically advantageous. The
highly qualified manpower that really mattered from this point of view
was the supply of technicians, engineers, and specialists in various other
applied fields. It therefore made sense to divert the campaign for equality
of opportunity in this direction, and consequently vocational options had
to be made as attractive as the "general" alternatives. The political parties
now agree on this. The more radical view taken by the *SPD* is that
vocational training should no longer be seen from a purely economic
standpoint: it aims therefore at introducing training centres outside the
industrial firms so that vocational education would become a sector of the
national education system and cease to be the private responsibility of
these firms. But this abolition of the "dual system" of apprenticeship
training on the job combined with part-time *Berufsschule* instruction is a
long-term aim. Short-term objectives are more modest involving such
changes as the substitution of "block release" for the existing day-release
system and an increase in the proportion of apprentices' time which is
spent at school. The *CDU*, on the other hand, is expressly committed to
the retention of the dual system, favouring the development of staged
training outlined earlier. But it is in agreement with the *SPD* on the more
immediate objectives of block release and increase in the school-based
instruction for apprentices. With these areas of agreement it appears likely
that the early steps in the reform of vocational education will not prove
particularly controversial. The more long-term aims of the *SPD*, however,
imply a more fundamental change in the balance of responsibility as
between government and industry.

CHAPTER 4

Landmarks of Post-war Education Policy

The earliest post-war developments in the Federal Republic consisted of a progression from somewhat bewildering diversity towards a degree of standardisation. In accordance with the policy of "restoration" (*Restauration*) the education system, when viewed as a whole, did not differ greatly from that of the Weimar Republic. The *Gymnasium* and the *Volksschule* followed well-established traditions, while the intermediate *Mittelschule*, later called *Realschule*, also had its precedents. Finally, the vocational schools and the apprenticeship system were still perfectly viable in their pre-war form. But though the general framework is clearly distinguishable there persisted a great variety of interpretations within it. The discrepancies ranged from the trivial to the significant. At one end of the scale were differences in nomenclature and in the ways of organising the school year; at the other were the measures taken in some *Länder* to restructure the system by extending the duration of common primary schooling from four to six years. In the early life of the Federal Republic the awareness of the differences became sharpened and brought with it a general desire to standardise practices. This desire was reinforced by growing political opposition to the changes that involved delaying selection for the *Gymnasium* and the *Mittelschule*. It found expression in the Düsseldorf Agreement of 1955 which set out to standardise practices among the *Länder*.

THE DÜSSELDORF AGREEMENT (1955)

The Düsseldorf Agreement was concluded by the *Kultusminister-konferenz* during a period of economic expansion and social stability, a time when the attitude to education as to many other features of national life could be summed up by the catch-phrase *Keine Experimente*. It will accordingly be seen from its contents as set out below that the measures were overwhelmingly of an administrative character. Indeed, this could be called the "administrative stage" of post-war education policy in the Federal Republic. It should be noted, incidentally, that Bavaria declined to be a signatory to the Agreement and that at this point the Saar had not yet become a member of the federation. All the other *Länder* were involved.

The first section, entitled "General Regulations", was concerned with the calendar. The school year was to begin on 1 April and to end on 31 March. Holidays were to be fixed primarily in accordance with educational criteria and were to total 85 days including those Sundays and public holidays which fell within the holiday period and excluding additional free days given for special reasons. The summer vacation was to be fixed roughly between 25 June and 15 September; for Bremen, Berlin, Hamburg, Hesse, Lower Saxony, and Schleswig-Holstein more in the first half; for the other *Länder* more in the second half of this period. The other main holidays were to be at Christmas and Easter, and further shorter holiday periods were permissible at Whitsun and in the autumn as well as individual days off which varied according to local conditions.

The second section was concerned with intermediate and secondary schools. The former were to be called *Mittelschulen,* while all schools which led to the *allgemeine Hochschulreife* came under the category of *Gymnasium*; these terms were either to replace or to be added to traditional nomenclature. The years of school attendance were to be numbered 1–13. The *Mittelschule* was to build on the primary stage, the *Grundschule*, and in its shortened form was to begin at the latest after the seventh year of the general elementary school, the *Volksschule*. In all cases the *Mittelschule* ended with year 10. Only one compulsory foreign language was to be taught in it, generally English, and this was to begin at the latest after one year of the course. As regards the *Gymnasium*, its "long form" was to be considered normal but a "short form" was also possible; both had the same objective and terminated at the end of year 13 with the leaving examination, known as the *Reifeprüfung* or *Abitur*. The long form began after the *Grundschule*, and if the transfer took place after six years of this instead of the more customary four, this was on condition that systematic foreign language instruction for at least four periods per week was provided over two years. The short form began at the latest after the seventh year in the *Volksschule* and had no pre-requisites as regards foreign languages. In all cases admission was on the basis of entrance examinations. The long form comprised three types – the classical, the modern languages, and the mathematics/natural sciences *Gymnasium*; only the latter two were permissible in the short form. As regards the languages that were taught, the classical *Gymnasium* began in year 5 with Latin, in year 7 a new foreign language, and in year 8 Greek was added. The modern languages and mathematics/natural sciences *Gymnasien* in the long form began in year 5 with English, adding Latin or French in year 7. Exceptionally a *Gymnasium* or a branch of a *Gymnasium* could begin with Latin or French as the first foreign language if a sufficient number of schools of the normal type were available in the locality. Where it was planned that a school should bifurcate into a modern languages and a mathematics/natural sciences branch, this was to take place in year 9. In the modern languages *Gymnasium* a third foreign language was to be taught from year 9. Where previously this bifurcation had taken place from year 11, such an arrangement could continue until the conclusion of the next Agreement; the same applied to the timing for beginning a third foreign language. In the short form the modern languages and mathematics/natural sciences *Gymnasien* began with English in the first year of the course. The second foreign language began in the six-year short form in the second year, and in the seven-year short form in the third year of the course. A third foreign language was not compulsory in the short forms. In so far as cases of hardship arose for upper secondary pupils as a result of migration from one *Land* to another, this Agreement notwithstanding, special consideration was to be given. Exemptions could be allowed in one examination subject provided that the requirements in another group of subjects were correspondingly increased. The new regulations for *Gymnasien* were to be implemented at the latest from Easter 1957 and established courses in those schools which did not conform were to be brought to an end. If for educational reasons experiments were conducted as exceptions to the regulations, the essential character of the official types of school had to be preserved.

A third section of the Agreement provided for the mutual recognition of school-leaving certificates, including supplementary examinations in Latin and Greek, among the *Länder* that were signatories. This applied also to professional teaching qualifications provided that the examinations were conducted in accordance with the relevant *Kultusministerkonferenz* agreements and was unconditional in the case of the final examination for *Volksschule* teachers. In the fourth section examination grading systems were standardised. For the total assessment in teacher training there were four grades of pass: excellent (*mit Auszeichnung bestanden*), good (*gut bestanden*), creditable pass (*befriedigend bestanden*), and pass (*bestanden*). For individual subjects the gradings were very good (*sehr gut*), good (*gut*), creditable (*befriedigend*), adequate (*ausreichend*), poor (*mangelhalft*), and weak (*ungenügend*). The same six-point scale was to be used for all school assessments. Finally, there was a section making provision for the co-ordination of the Agreement with the internal legislation of the individual *Länder*. It was to be binding for a ten-year period.

THE *RAHMENPLAN* (1959)

Although in the early 1950s the main preoccupation in education policy was with improvements in administrative arrangements of the kind undertaken in the Düsseldorf Agreement, there was, none the less, a desire to review the workings of the system in a more fundamental way and, as has already been seen, this led to the creation of the *Deutscher Ausschuss für das Erziehungs- und Bildungswesen* in 1953. The pronouncements of this Commission made little impression until it published its famous *Rahmenplan* (Outline Plan) in 1959.

The document began with a historical review pointing out that the various branches of the education system had developed extensively before any attempts were made to bring them into a structural relationship. It stressed a number of factors: the development in Prussia of a qualifications system based on examinations which was a significant influence in the shaping of the modern system; the growth of secondary education to the point where modern languages, mathematics, and natural sciences took their place alongside classics as major subject areas; the development of the intermediate schools some of which, like the *Gymnasien* in certain States, acquired their own preparatory institutions separate from the elementary schools; and, finally, how in particular in the rural districts these elementary schools did in fact serve as the normal preliminary stage before the transition to intermediate or secondary level. The aim of this historical sketch was to make clear how the three major types of school — full secondary, intermediate, and elementary — had grown up separately and corresponded to three fairly clearly defined socio-cultural sections of the population. It was then pointed out how various forces in the twentieth century had been operating to bring about modifications to such a rigid structure: social differences were no longer preordained, and in this more fluid situation it was taken for granted that equality of educational opportunity should be striven for. The achievements of the Weimar Republic in establishing the four-year common *Grundschule* for all and in developing the idea of *Aufbauschulen* were acknowledged and passing reference made to the failure of attempts at centralisation under National Socialism as well as to the uninformed efforts to influence developments on the part of the Occupation powers. And so to the contemporary period and what the Commission saw as its task: to weld the products of these diverse trends and influences into a systematic whole.

Having then proceeded to analyse the various ideas for reorganisation that had been circulating in and outside Germany in the post-war period, the authors of the plan declared their hand in the form of three fundamental themes:

(1) The different educational requirements which in accordance with its division of labour our society places on its succeeding generation and the differences in educational potential of this new generation make it obligatory to keep to three educational targets of our school system which are reached after periods of schooling which vary in length; one which links up with employment relatively easily, an intermediate one, and a higher one. The structure of the school system must make it possible to raise the sights and to make the targets correspond in such a way with the intellectual changes of our time that in each child fundamental human powers are not only awakened but educated for the purpose of taking up diverse tasks and responsibilities in the modern world. It must therefore open up the three educational paths and so order their relationship to one another and devote so much time to each individual that the educational content and methods that are appropriate for him can unfold in their respective ways.

(2) The obligation to create social justice and the increased need on the part of modern society for a more highly educated coming generation make it necessary to open to each child that path which

corresponds to his educational potential. The structure of the school system must allow all the abilities of children to be awakened and also to be tested out through more demanding tasks at the appropriate level in each case. The decision on the question in which way and to what stage the child is to be educated must be made dependent on distinctly recognisable assessments in this evaluative process.

(3) The structure of the school system must play its part in firmly maintaining the intellectual unity of the people in elementary fundamental experiences, exercises, and insights, and lay a broad common base for the awareness of this unity. At the same time it must provide space and time to enable the varying educational potential of children to be verified under constant conditions and assessed accordingly. Both of these aims are only possible if all children have a common school experience until the point is reached where the special character of the educational paths makes a separation into specific types of school imperative.

The Commission then declared its plan to be an attempt to arrive at a constructive synthesis of tendencies which had hitherto rested on only one or two of these principles but whose justification was limited by the fact that all three must be considered valid. In its recommendations it adopted a nomenclature that corresponded as far as possible to existing practice, but for several of the components of its suggested system new names had to be invented.

As the basis of the system the four-year common *Grundschule* was scarcely in dispute, so that the plan carried real interest only as regards year 5 onwards. It was here that the first innovation was advocated, namely the idea of keeping most children together for a further two years in a kind of observation or orientation stage to be known as the *Förderstufe*. With this concept the Commission was attempting to reconcile conservative and evolutionary tendencies. During these two years it was considered that there would be a greater opportunity than before to seek out individual talent and to collect more extensive evidence on which to base the subsequent choice of school. The teaching methods, it was stressed, were to be more in keeping with a primary than a secondary approach, avoiding premature contact with abstractions. It was not however by any means intended that the *Förderstufe* should simply be an extension of the primary school. A good deal was made of the danger that this might happen and at the other extreme that the degree of differentiation would be such as merely to perpetuate the existing state of affairs. Some grouping on the basis of ability and inclination was favoured but not at the expense of the unity of the two-year period and not to the degree that the atmosphere in the schools would be dominated by the requirements of the selection process at the end of year 6. As to the organisation, since two years was too short a period for the *Förderstufe* to be an entirely self-contained unit, it was recommended that it should be linked either to the *Grundschule* or the *Hauptschule* as the upper stages of the old elementary school were now to be called.

This transformation of the upper elementary classes into an independent institution was one of the major problems and priorities thrown up by the plan. In view of the developments expected in the rest of the system the Commission was very much aware of the danger to the morale of the *Hauptschule*. It attempted briefly to delineate its main tasks as being to develop basic skills – both mental and manual – to promote civic education, and to provide a stable frame of reference for young people who were less and less subject to educative forces in the family and more and more vulnerable to exploitation. An earlier publication of the Commission had declared that many young people leaving school at 14 were simply not in a fit state of preparation to meet the demands that awaited them in employment. A rise of one year in the school-leaving age was recommended immediately and the addition of a further year, making the total *Schulpflicht* ten years, was to be the aim for the near future. For the moment, however, it was the eloquent plea of the Commission that teachers and employers should concentrate their energies on finding a way of making the ninth school year more relevant to everyday life while yet ensuring that it remained schooling rather than apprenticeship.

To some extent the plan eventually to extend the *Hauptschule* to ten years constituted a threat to the *raison d'être* of the intermediate *Realschule*, for it was argued that a modern industrialised society required the entire school population to be educated to the level of the *mittlere Reife*, the leaving qualification of the *Realschule* and of the intermediate stage of the *Gymnasium*. None the less, the Commission stood by the latter's individual character and its capability of providing a more demanding education than the *Hauptschule*. Its distinctiveness *vis-à-vis* the

Gymnasium was also indicated; mathematics, physics, and chemistry were to be important elements in the curriculum, and in the teaching of them the emphasis was to be on their practical application. The leaving qualification was still to be termed the *mittlere Reife*, but this equation with the intermediate qualification obtained in the *Gymnasium* was not considered really satisfactory, and the plan looked ahead to the time when it would be replaced by a *Fachschulreife*, a term which conveyed the vocational flavour of the work of the *Realschule*. As for duration, it was the Commission's view that, just as the minimum school-leaving age needed to be raised in order to come to terms with modern educational demands, so, too, the *Realschule* course should be extended by one year, making a total of five years to follow the *Förderstufe*. The impracticality of this in the short term was, however, recognised, and the best that could be hoped for was that an optional year 11 would be introduced where possible.

As regards full-length secondary education, a very clear dualism constituted the leitmotiv of the Commission's thinking. On the one hand, the schools were required to meet the greatly increased need for well-qualified manpower; on the other, they were the guardians of traditional European culture and responsible for transmitting it to the new generation. As the document put it: "we urgently require a large educated cohort for the rapidly rising demands of the technological world but we must not buy our way into this world at the expense of our intellectual and historical dimension." In its structural recommendations the plan followed this line of thinking by proposing a division of the secondary sector into two kinds of school – modern and classical. The modern variant, retaining the name *Gymnasium*, was to build on the *Förderstufe*, and to a considerable degree was seen as a response to the need to increase the number of *Abiturienten* and to the accompanying shift of emphasis among many of these from education (*Bildung*) to training (*Ausbildung*). For the classical variant the new name of *Studienschule* was proposed; this type of school was concerned with the traditional culture based on the classical languages and was to recruit direct from the *Grundschule*. It was intended that it should accept only those considered likely to acquire the *Hochschulreife* and go on to university, but it was expected that a number of children of this level of ability would prefer the *Gymnasien* on account of the emphasis on modern languages or mathematics and science which they offered.

The plan also devoted a good deal of space to curricular issues. Where the secondary schools had traditionally been almost exclusively geared to university entrance requirements, it was now acknowledged that a sizeable proportion would quite legitimately wish to leave before completion of the full secondary course and that of those who did complete it only some would proceed to the university. The encyclopedic tradition which demanded the study of at least twelve subjects through the nine years of the old secondary school clearly needed to be modified. What the authors of the plan suggested was that this broad range of subjects should be pursued to the end of year 11 only, when the *mittlere Reife* would be awarded, and that in the two final years there should be much greater scope for differentiated programmes than previously, while avoiding excessive specialisation.

"In the *Oberstufe* the number of obligatory subjects is reduced; four of them are singled out as characteristic of the type of school. The system of obligatory subjects ensures that the introduction of flexibility into the *Oberstufe* does not lead to an individualistic version of the course adopted and that the dominant educational idea of the school does not give way in the *Oberstufe* to a specialised education. Alongside these each pupil chooses one optional academic subject from among those that remain. Here a special interest on the part of the pupil should come into play and lead him to performance above the average. He should learn to handle independently the tools of the worker who uses his intellect and also to cope with bigger tasks without help. Since for this, time for quiet private study is required, the pupils must limit themselves to one optional academic subject. The study of the optional subject is completed at the end of the eleventh school year. The sacrifice involved in this loss of time is compensated for by the fact that subjects which hitherto were not examined in the *Abitur* can as optional subjects be pursued to a higher standard than has been possible in the *Gymnasium* up to now. In the *Abitur* the written examination is in the four basic subjects. The optional subject is part of the oral examination."

Though in its arguments the *Rahmenplan* was a fundamentally conservative document it gave rise to a vigorous controversy. It became clear that the structural recommendations stood little chance of acceptance; the overwhelming mass of opinion was against the two-year post-ponement of entry to the *Gymnasium*. What the *Förderstufe* idea did achieve, however, was a general awareness of the care that should be taken over these two years. Though by and large children still continued to be admitted to the *Gymnasium* after four primary years, they were then usually regarded as being in an "observation and orientation" stage, and increasing care was taken to ensure that they did not suffer the bewilder-ment of being put in the hands of many different teachers and plunged too suddenly into methods of study for which they were psychologically not ready. Two elements in the plan were, however, adopted by the *Kultus-ministerkonferenz*. Firstly, it resolved to raise the school-leaving age by a year at once. Secondly, in the Saarbrücken Agreement of 1960 the proposals regarding the reduction of the curriculum in the upper forms of the *Gymnasium* were approved. It proved a somewhat controversial agree-ment, however, and not all the *Länder* were prepared to go very far in implementing it. In the end it left its mark more firmly on the *Abitur* examination than on the prescribed curriculum.

THE HAMBURG AGREEMENT (1964)

The Düsseldorf Agreement of 1955, it will be recalled, had been accepted as binding by the *Länder*, with the exception of Bavaria, for a ten-year period. Accordingly, towards the end of 1964 it was renegotiated at a meeting of the *Kultusministerkonferenz* in Hamburg. All the *Länder* including Bavaria were signatories to the new version known as the Hamburg Agreement.

In the "General Regulations" section the calendar was changed so that the school year would begin on 1 August instead of 1 April. This was a case of the other *Länder* changing to conform to the existing practice in Bavaria. Those children were eligible to begin their primary schooling who had reached the age of 6 by 30 June and the compulsory period of attend-ance was nine years. The total holidays permissible were redefined as 75 working days to which special days off could be added at the discretion of the authorities. The timing of summer holidays was slightly altered: they were to fall within the period 1 July–10 September and were to be staggered on a regional basis in accordance with an agreement to be concluded annually by the *Kultusministerkonferenz*.

The second section largely confirmed the terminology used in the Düsseldorf Agreement but substituted *Realschule* for *Mittelschule* and recognised the possibility of using the term *Förderstufe* or *Beobachtungsstufe* where years 5 and 6 constituted a comprehensive stage. Institutions for evening study leading to intermediate and secondary school-leaving certificates were to use the names *Abendrealschule* and *Abendgymnasium* respectively; the full-time *Kolleg* was also recognised. The Agreement touched on a sensitive issue in acknowledging the existence of a *fachgebundene Hochschulreife*, a university entrance qualification restricted to certain faculties only. The duration of courses in the various school types was then spelt out together with the *Sprachenfolge*; this remained as in the Düsseldorf Agreement with the exception that the third foreign language, compulsorily Greek in the classical *Gymnasium*, was not to begin till year 9. In contrast to the Düsseldorf document, the Hamburg version was prepared to countenance educational experiments which deviated from the orthodox pattern but they did require authorisation by the *Kultusministerkonferenz*.

The third section confirmed previous provision for the mutual recognition of qualifications and the fourth confirmed the scales of assessment. In a fifth and final section it was declared that the Agreement had been concluded initially for a five-year period with provision to review it annually thereafter. It has remained the recognisable basis of the school systems of the *Länder* although some new elements have been added as explained in the next chapter.

THE *STRUKTURPLAN* (1970)

The *Strukturplan für das Bildungswesen* of 1970 represented a climax to five years of study of educational problems on the part of the *Bildungsrat,* subsuming as it did the recommendations of earlier publications of that body, in particular the proposals regarding leaving qualifications (*Zur Neugestaltung der Abschlüsse im Sekundarschulwesen*) issued in 1969. Described by the then federal Minister of Education Hans Leussink as "the most progressive, all-embracing general plan for the educational system which we have ever had",[1] it has a strong claim to be considered the most mature and sensitive of modern policy documents. It

[1] *Education in Germany*, 4/70, p. 2.

set out to achieve continuity with those developments which were already under way, to establish the basic principles that underlay them, and to suggest in anything but a dogmatic tone the possible ways in which the aims and objectives might be realised.

For the theoretical underpinning of their work the authors of the plan turned to the federal and *Land* constitutions and emphasised the freedoms enshrined in them. These basic rights, it was stressed, applied equally to all citizens; all should be in a position to avail themselves of them and be prepared to allow others to do so. The aim of education was to make a reality of this lofty aspiration through the agency of parents and of the State. There was therefore an obligation that the education that was provided should contain common elements; aims, educational principles, and the academic nature of content and teaching methods were to be applied equally to all sectors of the school system. Thus it was no longer to be possible to speak of a dichotomy between an academic education that was *volkstümlich,* that is to say popular in the sense that it catered for the mass of the people in a non-academic fashion. Education was in all cases to promote the welfare of the "whole man".

This line of thinking led the *Bildungsrat* to the kernel of the problem of the traditional German education system. Whatever the arguments in favour of reorganisation through the creation of *Gesamtschulen,* the political constellations in the *Land* parliaments ruled this out on any nationwide basis. Yet there was no doubt whatsoever about the seriousness of the curricular problems thrown up by the tripartite system. Selection for different types of school had at the same time meant selection for different types of curriculum and for the great majority in the *Volksschule/Hauptschule* a curriculum that led to no recognised leaving qualification. The *Bildungsrat* set about its analysis of the school system primarily with this problem in mind. In the *Strukturplan* a new nomenclature was used to convey the idea of unified stages which at the secondary level embraced horizontally all the kinds of school and attempted to give them a form of common identity.

Following this scheme the pre-school stage was named *Elementarbereich,* while *Primarbereich* was the suggested term for the first four or six years of school attendance. As a long-term aim it was proposed that this compulsory attendance should begin at the age of 5, a year earlier than was the existing practice. The importance of pre-school education was one of the features particularly emphasised in the plan which contained an analysis of the principles according to which it should be conducted and an apologia for its provision on a large scale. The educational theories of the primary stage were also discussed and the section devoted to this echoed the growing feeling in the Federal Republic that more substantial academic content should be introduced here. It was a particular concern that years 5 and 6, the *Orientierungsstufe*, which was envisaged as eventually applying to the age range 9–11, should be a comprehensive stage in its own right and lose the compromise character of its predecessor the *Förderstufe*.

The lower secondary level was designated *Sekundarstufe I* and the upper secondary *Sekundarstufe II*. Assuming a rise in the school-leaving age, making the compulsory period of full-time attendance ten years for all, it became possible to talk in terms of an intermediate leaving qualification that could be awarded in all the kinds of school. It was suggested that this should be known as *Abitur I* and that all schools should offer the corresponding curriculum which would lead to it. This was to be made up of a common core of nine subjects, namely German, a foreign language, mathematics, science, civics, music, art, religious instruction, and physical education; these were to be the only subjects studied in the *Orientierungsstufe*. Thereafter additional time would be allotted to optional extra subjects, the range of which was to be extended. The *Sekundarstufe I* was thus to be characterised by gradually increasing differentiation.

At the upper secondary stage too the *Strukturplan* aimed to make provision for a greater flexibility of curriculum, again on the "core and course" principle. The proposals illustrate clearly the desire to break down the barriers between academic and vocational activities at this level. It was to be possible to acquire the suggested new leaving certificate, the *Abitur II,* in any of the types of school, the traditional *Gymnasium*, the newer types of specialised *Gymnasium*, the *Fachoberschule*, or the *Gesamtschule*. In general its reflections on upper secondary education provide a good illustration of the seminal quality of the *Strukturplan,* for the kind of flexibility it advocated is in the process of being realised as a result of the *Kultusministerkonferenz* decision on this matter in 1972. The *Strukturplan* thinking can be seen, too, in the *Bildungsgesamtplan* of 1973, though one or two of the more controversial terms had by then been dropped, in particular the use of the word *Abitur* for a qualification acquired at the intermediate level.

The *Strukturplan* also contained some sketchy observations on further education, particularly in respect of the need for co-operation between the various authorities and bodies concerned with it, and for a clearer statement of its place as an integral rather than a peripheral part of the education system. The plan also followed its recommendations through by analysing their implications for the training of teachers; the controversial proposals put forward are discussed in a later chapter.

THE *BILDUNGSBERICHT* (1970)

Subtitled the "Educational Thinking of the Federal Government" the 1970 Report on Education had the declared aim of setting in motion the discussions which it was hoped would culminate in agreement between the federal government and the *Länder* on a practical programme of reform. It looked forward to the *Bildungsgesamtplan* which the *Bund-Länder-Kommission* presented in 1973.

The main value of the document lay in its presentation in a convenient and readable form of an extensive factual analysis of the education system. Statistical tables and diagrams were included which illustrated among other things: the expansion that had taken place since 1950 and the changing patterns of distribution of pupils and students among the different sectors; the growth in expenditure on education from 7·5 per cent of the national budget in 1951 to 13·4 per cent in 1968, together with international comparisons of expenditure as a proportion of the Gross National Product, comparisons which showed the Federal Republic to be relatively less generous than all eight other countries listed, viz. the USA, France, Japan, Holland, Great Britain, Sweden, Belgium, and Italy; the social background of *Gymnasium* pupils in 1965 and the rise in the proportion obtaining the *Abitur* between 1957 and 1968 and obtaining the leaving certificate of the *Realschule* during the same period; international comparisons showing the numbers of children for whom pre-school education was being provided; teacher—pupil ratios in the various types of school; the proportion of girls, firstly, among *Gymnasium* pupils, which had risen from 39·8 to 42·5 per cent between 1960 and 1967, and, secondly, among those obtaining the *Abitur* at *Gymnasium* the figure for which had risen from 35·8 to 37·3 per cent over the same period; the proportion of girls among *Realschule* pupils which had remained fairly constant at around 52·5 per cent; the expansion of the vocational system, together with breakdowns of the numbers in different categories of apprenticeship; and developments in higher education in terms of numbers of students, average time required to complete a degree course, staff–student ratios, social background of students, and international comparisons of their numbers per 100,000 of population. In most cases the statistics were broken down by *Land*, thus giving an interesting picture of the variegated pattern of provision within the federation.

The *Bildungsbericht* was primarily an information and opinion-forming exercise whereby the central government hoped to arouse among the general public sufficient awareness of educational issues to guarantee the necessary political support for the reforms which it wished to carry through.

THE *BILDUNGSGESAMTPLAN* (1973)

While the work of the *Bildungsrat* continued beyond the *Strukturplan*, exploring various other issues such as the reorganisation of the administration of education, another body was set up in 1970, the *Bund-Länder-Kommission für Bildungsplanung*, the main task of which was to relate the new thinking on the development of the system to specific quantitative forecasting and costing. In the first three years of its existence the Commission prepared a fresh *Rahmenplan* and an educational budget for it which together made up the document known as the *Bildungsgesamtplan*. This was the first essay in detailed long-term forecasting which had been undertaken on a federal basis, and the authors of the plan were careful to indicate their awareness of the pitfalls. None the less, it was felt to be necessary to indulge in the exercise in order to come to terms with five major urgent problems identified as a result of discussions with the various interested parties. These priorities were: improvements in pre-school education; vocational education at the upper secondary level; the introduction of an orientation stage (a descendant of the *Förderstufe*); the supply of teachers; and the expansion of capacity in higher education.

In pre-school education (the *Elementarbereich*) the aim was to provide places in kindergartens for all three- and four-year-olds whose parents wished it. Not only was the provision of places to be greatly increased but the facilities in terms of space and equipment were to be improved. As regards five-year-olds, at the time the plan was drawn up it was still un-certain whether they would eventually be regarded as part of the primary age group or whether they would remain within the compass of the kinder-garten. The decision regarding this was to await the outcome of various experimental arrangements. Either way, however, the aim was to achieve 100 per cent provision by 1985. For the primary stage significant improve-ments in facilities and teaching methods were anticipated, helped in particular by a favourable development in the staff—pupil ratio.

Beyond the primary level the *Bildungsgesamtplan* followed the approach of the *Strukturplan* in comprehending all types of post-primary school within the concepts of Secondary I and Secondary II. Secondary I (*Sekundarbereich I*) comprised all varieties of full-time education up to the end of the ninth or tenth year. While it was acknowledged that for the moment many pupils would continue to leave school at the end of the ninth year, it was expected that more and more would complete ten, and so reach the stage of the intermediate leaving qualification. At lower secondary level the idea of a compulsory common core curriculum together with a steadily increasing range of options was strongly supported. At this point the division over the question of the *Gesamtschule* became clear, for the plan stated:

"The federal government and six *Länder* take the view that these principles require the organisational form of the integrated *Gesamtschule*. While the other five *Länder* also subscribe to the principles they are not convinced that the integrated *Gesamtschule* is the best way to achieve the objectives. They believe that in a dif-ferentiated school system there are better prospects of guaranteeing the promotion of varying talents. For that reason they consider a decision on the future structure of the *Sekundarbereich I* to be possible only after the completion of the experimental programme of integrated and co-operative *Gesamtschulen* undertaken by the *Kultusminister-konferenz* alongside the continued development of the differentiated system."

The same division among the *Länder* was apparent over the question of the orientation stage in the first two secondary years in that one group wished to see it develop as an independent entity within a comprehensive structure while the other considered it possible to implement the idea within the existing types of school.

The leitmotiv of the *Strukturplan,* it will be recalled, was to ensure that all children were given the opportunity to acquire a recognised leaving certificate at the end of year 10. This was again stressed in the *Bildungs- gesamtplan,* and it was the intention that it should also be possible for those who left school after nine years to obtain the certificate after a further year of general vocational training, the so-called *Berufsgrundbild- ungsjahr.* The idea of this was to avoid premature entry to specialised apprenticeships, but it remains an area of controversy between education authorities and industrial and commercial interests.

For the upper secondary level (*Sekundarbereich II*) the *Bildungs- gesamtplan* attempted, as the *Strukturplan* had done, to create the impression of a comprehensive flexible framework within which the various types of education and training were all interrelated. The guiding principles for future development were defined as follows:

All sectors of *Sekundarbereich II* should be so structured as to offer the individual pupil the possibility of placing emphasis on those aspects of his education which correspond to his inclinations and abilities.

The establishment of parity of value between vocational and general education is an urgent political task. It demands a reordering and expansion of the vocational education system as well as the further development of the *gymnasiale Oberstufe* in the agreed differentiated form.

The curricula in the existing general and vocational education systems should be more closely co-ordinated with one another as regards content.

The theoretical aspect of those programmes which lead directly to a vocational qualification and employment should be expanded and their variety increased without abandoning their close relationship to practical work. This applies particularly where the training is partly in school, partly during employment.

The training facilities of small and medium-sized firms are often limited. Special importance should therefore be attached to the further development of training centres independently of them.

Curricula of comparable value which at present receive separate assessments in the general and vocational education systems and lead to different qualifications should be placed on the same level in this respect.

Courses which as well as furnishing a vocational qualification also open the way to higher education should be more extensively developed.

Ways of drawing the different varieties of education and training together should be tried out in model experiments and in the course of these the isolation of the part-time *Berufsschule* is to be avoided.

Young people with no leaving certificate should be offered appropriate educational opportunities.

The new structure of courses in the *Sekundarbereich II* demands a reorganisation of leaving certificates and the qualifications that accompany them. Each leaving certificate will in its "profile" reflect the type, content, and scope of the individual course that has been successfully pursued.

Schools are responsible for conferring the right to further study. In subjects where there are entrance restrictions for higher education, special conditions must be fulfilled by all candidates.

Depending on the type and scope of his course the individual pupil will as a rule spend two or three years in the *Sekundarbereich II*.

There should be provision for special education for the handicapped to take place either in special schools (*Sonderschulen*) or within the normal school system. The two spheres are to be as closely co-ordinated as possible.

In addition to setting out these principles for the development of schools the *Bildungsgesamtplan* pronounced on the future of higher education and the training of teachers. This part of the plan is discussed in Chapter 7.

CHAPTER 5

The School System

Some indication has already been given in earlier chapters of the
complexity of the school system of the Federal Republic. The many
additions of the post-war period have given a baroque effect that tends to
obscure the main features of the edifice. In a survey such as the one which
follows it is no longer enough to make an inventory of the different types
of school – it is also necessary to take account of the new horizontal
structure, seen in terms of an examinations and qualifications system, that
is being superimposed on the original tripartite pattern which has displayed a remarkable durability in the context of widespread change in
western Europe.[1]

PRIMARY AND PRE-SCHOOL EDUCATION

THE PRE-SCHOOL SECTOR

Pre-school education in the form of kindergartens has in the past been
mainly provided not by the State but independently of it by churches,
industrial and commercial companies, or through private enterprise on the
part of individuals. It has become a major growth area in educational
provision. The demand for places greatly ·exceeds the supply and is
growing steadily, partly on account of the increase in the number of
married women in employment, partly because of a general recognition of
the importance of group activity for three- to six-year-olds, and the

---

[1] This survey draws in a number of places on W. Schultze and C. Führ, *Das
Schulwesen in der Bundesrepublik Deutschland,* 3rd edn., Weinheim, 1973, q.v. for an
exhaustive catalogue of current practice.

bearing which education at this stage has on subsequent performances at primary school and later. As a consequence of this there has been a rising interest in and encouragement of further development by federal and *Land* authorities, aimed at increasing the number of institutions, improving facilities and equipment, and providing more and better-trained teachers. In the planning of the future development of the school system, pre-school education has acquired the designation "elementary domain" (*Elementarbereich*), indicating that it is now officially regarded as a major phase in its own right. According to the federal plan of 1973 it is expected that 70 per cent of three- and four-year-olds will be receiving some kind of schooling by 1985. The new emphasis on education at this level has affected the work of the kindergartens in that there is a desire to be more methodical about laying foundations for the work of the primary stage. While this does not imply systematic instruction in the three Rs in kinder-garten, there is no doubt that more and more five-year-olds are ready for such instruction and are for this reason being admitted to primary schools at an earlier age than was the case in the past.

THE PRIMARY SECTOR

The formal school year begins in August when the new entry is made up of those children who had reached the age of 6 by the end of the previous June. It is, however, also possible for those who are considered sufficiently advanced to be admitted up to six months earlier than this provided that the school medical authorities give their consent. This recent extension evidences a general trend towards an earlier start to formal education; the federal plan of 1973 advocates primary school from the age of 5, to be introduced by stages and completed by 1985. The primary stage spans the first four years of formal school attendance except in West Berlin and the "city states" of Hamburg and Bremen where there is a six-year primary school. In the latter two cases, however, some children do transfer to the *Gymnasium* after four years. Throughout the Federal Republic the offical term for primary school is *Grundschule*, but where it takes a four-year form its separation from the secondary stage is not always distinct since it is in many cases combined with the non-selective secondary school, the *Hauptschule*. Where this is so the older term *Volksschule* often remains in use to cover both. This also means, of course, that many children receive their entire full-time education in one and the same institution.

However, though not always organisationally distinct, the primary school is a self-contained unit from the point of view of curriculum. Traditionally all instruction has been given by a class teacher cast in the "village schoolmaster" mould. According to this stereotype the teaching was of a non-academic kind, strongly emphasising German history and geography together with knowledge of the more immediate local environ-·ment, and with a certain homeliness about it which was intended to engender national feeling. This unambitious programme was the product of a time when only a small minority would subsequently face the more rigorous demands of the *Gymnasium* from the age of 10. The expansion of more recent years has made this approach outdated, and the *Kultus-ministerkonferenz* has made it clear that *Grundschule* teaching must be greatly strengthened in order to guarantee greater equality of opportunity and a sounder basis for later work in the *Hauptschule*, the *Realschule*, or the *Gymnasium*. The more systematic approach that is now required has led to the growing introduction of subject specialist teaching especially in mathematics but also in the mother tongue, music, art, and physical education. In some *Länder* English is being taught experimentally during the third and fourth primary years. But for all this desire to improve the grounding in individual disciplines there is at the same time a concern to retain as far as possible the advantages of having one member of staff with clearly defined overall responsibility for each class and some *Land* regulations stipulate a minimum daily time to be allowed for instruction by the class teacher.

PRIMARY – SECONDARY TRANSFER

The evolution of the German school system has been cautious, characterised by a reluctance to tamper with tradition; the desire to broaden opportunities has been accompanied by a disinclination to alienate those groups with a strong commitment to long-established structures and practices. Since the transition from primary to secondary education involves a choice of alternatives with far-reaching implications, the procedures involved have been subjected to close scrutiny. After the *Rahmenplan* a number of *Länder*, most noticeably Hesse, experimented with the idea of the *Förderstufe* which was advanced in it. This did not affect the selection of the more able after four years of primary school, but rather was designed to ensure that the prospects of the remainder were not written off. The first two years in the *Hauptschule* were looked upon as a unit and, to further the prospects of transition to a *Realschule* or a *Gymnasium*, at the end of this period children were grouped by ability for instruction in German, mathematics, and a foreign language. But it should be emphasised that the *Förderstufe* was an experiment and a far from extensive one at that.

Concern over procedures involving selection at the age of 10 remained, and in 1966 the *Kultusministerkonferenz* addressed itself to the problem of establishing what was appropriate for each individual child at the secondary stage. According to their statement, consultation with parents was to start at the beginning of the last primary year when a provisional opinion would be expressed by teachers. Towards the end of the year a total profile of the child was to be prepared which would include specific evidence of achievement. Meetings between teachers and parents were then to be held at which the various possibilities would be discussed. As a further measure provision was made for aptitude and achievement tests to be carried out by way of pieces of written work and a period of "trial teaching" (*Probeunterricht*). It was expressly pointed out that though the latter was to be conducted by secondary teachers it was to be based on the work done in the primary school, and those responsible were to discuss methods of going about it with their primary colleagues. But the *Länder* were left free to dispense with these procedures where the staff of the primary school made an unqualified recommendation for transfer to a particular type of secondary education. Where the procedures were adopted it was stressed that the teaching groups should be small, the atmosphere characterised by "quietness and kindness", and the work spaced out over a reasonable period. The entire process was to come under the jurisdiction of a committee on which both primary and secondary schools were represented and which had the task of reconciling the views expressed in the primary school report with the general impression made in the tests and the *Probeunterricht*. Differences of opinion, it was emphasised, were to be settled by discussion among the parties concerned. Transfer was to be provisional and reviewed at the end of the first year in the new school so that mistakes could be corrected.

It is on the basis of this statement that the current picture of transfer has emerged. Examinations of the old kind for assessing attainment have disappeared entirely and intelligence and aptitude tests have ceased to feature greatly. The primary school report or "profile" has become the most influential factor, and in most *Länder* suffices as grounds on which to make decisions. Usually the function of the *Probeunterricht* is to serve as a basis for adjudication in cases where the parents' wishes and the primary school recommendation are at variance. Exceptionally though, in West Berlin it is the parents who have the final say. As had been the case with the *Förderstufe*, the first two years at a *Gymnasium* or a *Realschule* are now generally regarded as a unit. The probationary period after selection is therefore generally of two years' duration, and children cannot be kept back at the halfway stage. Since the publication of the *Strukturplan* of 1970 and more recently as a result of the work of the *Bund-Länder-Kommission*, it has been an official target to reach a situation where the full range of provision during the two-year period will be available to all. This is the concept of the *Orientierungsstufe* in which there would be no segregation into different schools, and ability grouping would be confined to mathematics and a foreign language. The *Länder* are currently working to reach agreement on the curriculum for this period. The *Orientierungsstufe* can obviously enough be most conveniently realised as part of a comprehensively structured system. But in most of the Federal Republic it is necessary to reckon with the continued existence of *Gymnasien* and *Realschulen*. This therefore raises the problem of whether a common *Orientierungsstufe* should be incorporated in the primary sector or organised as a separate middle stage – a nettle that remains to be grasped.

The transitional period is marked by the striving for co-operation, firstly, between primary and secondary teachers, and, secondly, between teachers as a whole and parents. If the general picture is one of conservative adherence to the principle of segregation by ability, there is, too, a patent desire to ensure that selection should take place under humane circumstances and a general acceptance that the children should always be given the benefit of any doubt. Opportunities for transfer at later stages are increasing, and it would appear that cases where children wishing to enter a *Gymnasium* or a *Realschule* are unable to do so are rare. The problem in Germany has long been the reluctance of able working-class children to opt for anything other than the minimum full-time education of a non-academic kind. None the less, as the recruitment to the *Gymnasium* and the *Realschule,* which in the 1970s has been upwards of 35 per cent of the age cohort, continues to increase, there could well result a substantial growth in the representation from the lower socio-economic levels. And clearly the implementation of the idea of an orientation stage for years 5 and 6, though still some way in the future, could accelerate such a trend.

SECONDARY EDUCATION

THE *HAUPTSCHULE*

The problem of the *Hauptschule* has been to shed the inherited character of the senior section of the elementary school and establish its own identity as a separate form of secondary education. This aim of independence is best served when there is a physical separation from the *Grundschule*, and this process is under way in both urban and rural areas. In the former case there is more scope for flexibility in the reallocation of buildings, and reorganisation is therefore easier. Where the population is more sparsely distributed it has been necessary to set up central schools (*Mittelpunktschulen*) with a catchment area embracing a number of village primary schools. Formerly the obstacle to this kind of rationalisation was the survival of single denomination schools especially in rural areas of Bavaria, Baden-Württemberg, Rhineland-Palatinate, the Saar, and North Rhine-Westphalia. However, the development of mixed schools in those areas has recently been eased by legislation which has succeeded in re-conciling the conflicting interests involved.

The curriculum of the *Hauptschule* comprises the predictable elements of German, history, geography, social studies, mathematics, physics, chemistry, biology, music, art, and physical education. Two further components illustrate its particular objectives. The first is the foreign language, usually English but in some cases French. The building up of language teaching has been a way of ensuring that the *Hauptschule* can operate in genuine parallel with other secondary schools and therefore cease to be a "blind alley". Previously the lack of such instruction had made subsequent entry to the *Realschule* or the *Gymnasium* impossible. All *Hauptschulen* now take their pupils to the end of the ninth school year, and in a growing number a tenth year is possible with a leaving certificate that can be equated with that of the *Realschule*. The second significant element is *Arbeitslehre* or "practical instruction". The idea that this should make an important contribution to the character of the *Hauptschule* goes back to the *Rahmenplan* and subsequent recommendations of the *Deutscher Ausschuss*. There followed a pronouncement by the *Kultusministerkonferenz* in 1969 which stated that the subject should "impart the insights, knowledge, and skills in the technico-economic and socio-political spheres which are today necessary elements in the basic education of every citizen; promote afresh co-operative activity; give assistance in the choice of a career, though stopping short of providing vocational education". These objectives have been endorsed by other groups interested in vocational education, and some have advocated its extension to the *Realschule* and the *Gymnasium*, and, as will be seen in the next chapter, it is a particular preoccupation of those concerned with curriculum development in the *Gesamtschule* context. At present experimental programmes are in progress designed to establish what components the syllabus for *Arbeitslehre* should comprise. The eventual evaluation of these projects will no doubt make for interesting comparisons with the polytechnical education long established in the *DDR*.

Such ideas reflect a growing feeling that general and vocational education have become too separated from one another, and certainly whatever can be done to break down the barriers between them will be of benefit to the *Hauptschule* which is in danger of being torn in two directions, on the one hand, the quest for an academic respectability comparable to that of the other secondary schools, and, on the other, the challenge to experiment with new ideas which aim to give a broader general education of an appropriate kind to those who appear more likely to go directly into vocational training after school. Implied in the statements about the *Hauptschule* is the hope that it will acquire its prestige by the latter route but yet that this will not deny prospects of a more academic option to those pupils who desire it.

THE *REALSCHULE*

The *Realschule*, formerly known as the *Mittelschule*, can be loosely described as a semi-academic intermediate school spanning years 5–10 of school attendance or years 7–10 where there is a six-year primary school. Since the creation of the Federal Republic there has been a large expansion in the numbers of schools in this category, somewhere between three- and fourfold in the period up to 1969 when the proportion of the thirteen-year-old cohort in *Realschulen* was 18 per cent. One significant reason for this increase has been that for many parents, the *Realschule* has seemed more acceptable as a means of advancement for their children than the more academic *Gymnasium*. It has been considered an appropriate preparation for subsequent training courses in such fields as welfare, catering, nursing, or engineering to technician level, and in general has been closely geared to career opportunities in industry, commerce, administration, and agriculture. More recently the possibilities of transfer at the end of the course to the upper classes (*Oberstufe*) of the *Gymnasium* have been greatly improved, though the majority of pupils choose a more directly vocational option at this stage. This range of opportunities has greatly promoted the popularity of the *Realschule*, and the expansion that the sector has experienced has been perhaps the principal response to the demand for a broadening of educational opportunity at the secondary level.

The curriculum of the *Realschule* reflects the prominence given to vocational considerations, but also provides the orthodox general range of subjects, religious instruction, German, history, geography, civics, current affairs, mathematics, physics, chemistry, biology, art, music, physical education, and one or two foreign languages. In the later years of the course additional options are offered such as economics, bookkeeping and accountancy, shorthand and typing, technical drawing, woodwork, and metalwork. There is a growing degree of differentiation by ability and inclination, making it possible to intensify the teaching of, for example, mathematics, physics, and technical drawing, or of modern languages, especially in cases where transfer to a *Gymnasium* is sought.

THE *GYMNASIUM*

The *Gymnasium* is the academic secondary school which has traditionally prepared its pupils primarily for entrance to university with a nine-year course (years 5–13 of school attendance) or a seven-year one where there is a six-year primary school (years 7–13). After the war three main types were re-established, the classical (*altsprachliches Gymnasium*), the modern languages (*neusprachliches Gymnasium*), and the mathematics/natural sciences (*mathematisch-naturwissenschaftliches Gymnasium*), but other variants have gradually appeared so that the present picture is a complex one. Whereas the leaving certificate of the traditional types conferred the right to pursue any kind of higher education including entry to any faculty of any university (*allgemeine Hochschulreife*), with some of the newer institutions this right is restricted to certain courses (*fachgebundene Hochschulreife*). The distinction is one of curriculum. The older types of *Gymnasium* could claim the polyvalence of their leaving qualification on the grounds that their curriculum spanned a very wide range of academic disciplines; the newer institutions had a narrower scope. But the distinction has become less sharp as a result of measures to reduce the burden on pupils in the senior *Gymnasium* classes by introducing a greater flexibility and a degree of specialisation throughout the upper secondary sector. This process is an extension of a general drive to play down the differences between various types of secondary school and to emphasise what is common to all of them. At the lower secondary level, officially designated as *Sekundarstufe I*, the *Bildungsrat* has striven to reduce the curricular differences between the *Hauptschule*, the *Realschule*, and the *Gymnasium* by identifying a "common core" known as *Curriculum I*. The *Kultusministerkonferenz*, too, has taken steps to reduce differences of curriculum within the *Gymnasium* sector itself.

The *Gymnasium* curriculum has always been uncompromisingly academic with a particularly strong bias towards languages and literature. On the other hand, it has been far from easy to guarantee that even one foreign language is taught in the *Hauptschule*. Hence, in order to ensure that transfer from one type of school to the other is possible at the end of the two-year *Orientierungsstufe*, only one foreign language is taught in *Gymnasien* during this period. The second foreign language is introduced from year 7, and this applies also in the case of the seven-year *Gymnasium*, for six-year primary schools are obliged to provide instruction in a foreign language in their last two years. The first foreign language is, as a rule, English, or occasionally French in regions like the Saar which border on French-speaking territory, but in the classical *Gymnasium* it is always Latin. To this extent, therefore, a choice is made at the outset of secondary education, but it is intended that it should not be irrevocable, and failure to begin Latin at this point, year 5, does not preclude later study of classics. Greek is not taught till year 9 and is open to those who have studied Latin in years 7 and 8 only, as well as to those who began it earlier. The discrepancy over Latin is, however, an exception, for in all other respects the curricula of the three main *Gymnasium* types are very similar for the first four years.

Thereafter their specific character becomes more apparent. Though the classical *Gymnasium* is primarily concerned with Latin and Greek language and culture, a modern language is compulsory for all, and frequently French is offered as an alternative to Greek. The modern languages *Gymnasium* is particularly concerned with English and French language and culture, but Latin may be substituted for French, and often a third foreign language such as Russian, Spanish, or Italian is available. Though in the mathematics and natural sciences *Gymnasium* less emphasis is obviously placed on languages, none the less two are taught to all pupils, generally English and French, sometimes English and Latin. But it is these complexities of the patterns of languages studied, the *Sprachenfolge* as it is termed, that account for most of the individuality of the three *Gymnasium* types, and attention should not therefore be distracted from their remarkable homogeneity as a group, characterised by a long-established commitment to the tradition of a broad, general education. In the *Oberstufe* of all three types the curriculum includes religious instruction, German, civics, history, geography, mathematics, natural science, music or art, and physical education, though not all are pursued throughout the three years. This formidable common core has in the past given the *Abitur* both prestige and polyvalence, but this high reputation was also the product of a time when the *Oberstufe* of the three types had an unchallenged monopoly of upper secondary pre-university studies and a well-initiated clientele that accepted the cultural assumptions of the Humboldt tradition. The erosion of these conditions is the main current development in German education at this level.

One indication of the evolution that has taken place is the steady proliferation of new types of *Gymnasium*. In view of the difficulty of late transfer from a *Hauptschule* or a *Realschule* into a *Gymnasium* a special kind of school was created to provide an accelerated course in which those who had missed the normal entry could make up the lost ground and reach *Abitur* level. This kind of institution was known as the *Aufbaugymnasium* or *Gymnasium in Aufbauform*. A substantial number of them were started in North Rhine-Westphalia from 1965 on and were originally known as *Fachgymnasien* or *F-Gymnasien* because they led to a *fachgebundene Hochschulreife* (restricted access to higher education). More recently it has become not uncommon for them to grant the full *Hochschulreife* and the term *F-Gymnasium* has tended to go out of use. There are various stages at which such schools can begin but they are most commonly three-year upper secondary institutions (years 11–13 of school attendance). They may either be self-contained or organisationally linked to orthodox *Gymnasien* and, though originally designed mainly to pursue the latter's curricula after a late start, they have greatly widened the range of specialisms they offer and are increasingly drawing their intake from all branches of lower secondary education including the main types of *Gymnasium*. Thus a category had developed which now embraces a wide variety of specialised upper secondary schools. The specialisms are:

(i) Economics and business studies (*Wirtschaftswissenschaftliches Gymnasium*). This kind of school is found throughout the Federal Republic but has been particularly extensively developed in Baden-Württemberg.

(ii) Social studies (*Sozialwissenschaftliches Gymnasium*). This type exists in most *Länder*, especially Bavaria, and is mainly for girls. The new elements which it has brought into the school curriculum are drawn from law, economics, and social welfare and administration, and there is an emphasis on practical social work.

(iii) Technology (*Technisches Gymnasium* or *Technische Oberschule*). These schools combine theory and practice in the study of technology and are found in one form or another in all *Länder*.

(iv) The arts (*Musisches Gymnasium*). All pupils of this type study both music and the visual arts, one as a major, the other as a minor specialism. They provide special facilities for orchestral and choral work and are found in about half of the *Länder*.

(v) Sport (*Sportgymnasium*). This is a small category found in North Rhine-Westphalia and beginning in year 9. Sport accounts for seven or eight periods per week, replacing the third foreign language.

(vi) Educational studies (*Erziehungswissenschaftliches Gymnasium*). These schools, too, are rare, originating in North Rhine-Westphalia. Again it is the third foreign language which has made way for education as a subject.

(vii) Agriculture (*Landwirtschaftsgymnasium*). A few schools with this specialism are provided in Baden-Württemberg and Lower Saxony.

(viii) Domestic science (*Hauswirtschaftsgymnasium*). In this and other variously named girls' schools, e.g. the *Frauenberufliches Gymnasium*, are offered not only domestic science but other options already listed such as the arts and educational studies, in addition to the orthodox academic choices.

A further indication of the evolution of secondary education is afforded by the efforts to reshape the curriculum of the more orthodox *Gymnasien*. The pressure exerted on pupils by the demands of the traditionally encylopedic programme that was compulsory for all had long been a cause for concern. But the various initiatives designed to introduce greater flexibility and to allow an element of specialisation had largely been unsuccessful. The principal reason for this was that *Gymnasium* teachers did not find it easy to accept the increased scope for independent study which was the natural concomitant of specialisation. For this involved departure from a tradition of formal instruction, factual learning, and close supervision of all school activity; the idea of private study or project work, for example, was rarely explored. The issue was seen clearly enough. As early as 1951 a study group engaged on this problem had coined the phrase *Arbeiten Können ist mehr als Vielwisserei* (the ability to work is more important than the accumulation of knowledge). Yet when the opportunity was provided to make reductions in the curriculum under the terms of the Saarbrücken Agreement of the *Kultusministerkonferenz* in 1960, it was regarded in the *Gymnasium* sector and in the universities as an unacceptable dilution of the tradition of *Allgemeinbildung*. Changes were in fact introduced in a few *Länder* but they did not remain in operation for long.

The malaise continued, however, and gradually the need for change became more widely acknowledged. One significant factor was a growing feeling in the universities that standards of attainment in the *Gymnasium* were declining and that the school-leaving certificate, the *Abitur,* was no longer the guarantee of fitness for university study (*Studierfähigkeit*) that it had formerly been. It was a matter of opinion whether this was due to the explosion of knowledge which caused excessive demands to be made, or to the explosion of numbers which brought a reduction in the average level of ability, or to work-shyness among pupils exposed to many more external distractions than in the past, or to some permutation of these. At all events the gradual acceptance of a need for change took concrete form in 1972 through an agreement of the *Kultusministerkonferenz* on the subject (*Vereinbarung zur Neugestaltung der gymnasialen Oberstufe in der Sekundarstufe II*). The provisions of this Agreement were to be implemented by the school year 1976/7.

It is an aim of the new Agreement, therefore, to provide greater scope for the individual abilities and interests of pupils and for the exercise of individual responsibility in the making of choices, an approach which seeks to acknowledge the increased independence of the 16–19 age group that has been evident in recent years. It is, further, an attempt to improve preparation for university so that entrants will have a clearer idea of their academic aspirations. In the past it was not at all unusual to postpone a serious beginning to university study until some time after entry. But the increasing pressure to reduce the duration of university studies makes this dilatoriness no longer acceptable. This trend towards more serious consideration of vocation at upper secondary level is an inevitable byproduct of the greatly increased competition for admission to universities, evidenced by the need to operate a *numerus clausus* in many faculties. Where once the *Abitur* automatically guaranteed entry it is now necessary to apply a quota system whereby only a percentage of applicants are accepted directly from school, while the remainder must wait their turn and while doing so take up some other occupation which is sufficiently appropriate to enhance their prospects of acceptance at a later date. With a bottleneck of this kind in existence the need to streamline the organisation of the pre-university stage has been obvious. It is hoped that by forcing upper secondary pupils to be clear about their intentions, the new measures will induce some to think seriously about a wider range of career opportunities rather than to follow the traditional course of going to university virtually automatically. Where the *Abitur* was formerly regarded almost exclusively aa a university entrance examination it is intended that this should be only one aspect of its role in the future; its function should rather be that of a school-leaving certificate, leading not only to university but to a range of alternative vocational opportunities. In view of this the former distinctions between the three main types of *Gymnasium* – classical, modern languages, and mathematics/natural sciences – and the more specialist types enumerated earlier are likely to disappear as all institutions acquire the new collective identity of an upper secondary stage, the *Sekundarstufe II* as it is termed in the plans of the *Bildungsrat* and the *Bund-Länder-Kommission.*

The Agreement signals the final breakdown at the upper secondary level of the *Jahrgang* principle according to which each class is kept together as a unit for all subjects throughout its progress through the school. The new arrangement seeks to individualise studies by means of a system of half-year course units with differentiation on the basis of ability and achievement. The curriculum is divided into five areas:

(i) The linguistic, literary, and aesthetic domain – the study of the mother tongue, linguistic structures, taking account of different registers and levels of communication; at least one foreign language; course in literature, music, and the visual arts, designed to promote understanding of creative work and human endeavour, including its sociological aspects.

(ii) The social sciences – the study of appropriate multidisciplinary themes to promote understanding of historical, political, social, geographical, economic, and legal subject matter, and especially social change in the industrial age and contemporary international relations.

(iii) Mathematics, natural sciences, and technology – the study of the process of abstraction and logical argument, accuracy of calculation, mathematical thinking, the study of the scientific method, the development of models and their application to organic and inorganic structures, the study of theories in the natural sciences.

(iv) Religious education – the presentation of the foundations on which the relevant religious community is built, the study of questions of meaning and value in life, confrontation with other religions, ideologies and philosophies, the promotion of responsible action in society.

(v) Physical education.

All of these areas are represented in a common core of studies for all pupils with at least three periods per week devoted to German, mathematics, and foreign languages and totalling some two-thirds of the curriculum. The remainder is given over to specialised courses which either involve more advanced study of the common core subjects or less traditionally orthodox options such as education, psychology, sociology, law, geology, astronomy, technology, statistics, computer science, and others to be added in the future. The flexibility of the half-year course unit system makes it possible for the upper secondary studies leading to the *Abitur* to be completed over two, three, or four years. With the disappearance of the *Jahrgang* principle the idea of a form teacher (*Klassenlehrer*) gives way to that of a personal tutor (*Beratungslehrer*) to advise on appropriate choices.

Under the new dispensation the *Abitur* and the *allgemeine Hochschulreife* are awarded on the basis of three equal components: the work of the final two years in the common core subjects, the work of the final two years in the specialist subjects, and the results of terminal examinations. The latter involve written papers in two specialist subjects and in one common core subject other than these two; additional oral tests in these three where desirable; an oral examination in one subject other than these three, or, alternatively, in certain circumstances a test in physical education. The traditional grading system from 1 down to 6 is retained, but for computation of *Abitur* results there is a conversion into marks covering a range from 15 down to zero. The maximum marks that can be achieved in each of the three components is 300, so that the final *Abitur* score is out of a maximum of 900. The wide range of differentiation that this provides could greatly facilitate decisions regarding admissions to university faculties where the number of places available is limited. There is, however, a deeply rooted aversion to the idea that transition from school to university should be regulated by arithmetical means, and it must therefore be doubtful whether there will ever be recourse to such *Notenarithmetik* on an extensive scale.

The 1972 Agreement represents without doubt the most far-reaching proposal for change at upper secondary level since the war. At present it is being tried out experimentally in selected schools and it is to be fully implemented throughout the Federal Republic by the school year 1976/7.

ALTERNATIVES IN PRIVATE AND ADULT EDUCATION

Various alternatives to the State system exist in the form of private schools. The right to set these up is guaranteed in the Constitution and they are subsidised to varying and mostly very generous degrees by the *Länder.* The most numerous by far are the denominational schools, in particular the Roman Catholic ones which are generally boarding establishments, many of them exclusively for girls. Protestant private schools are less common. Some boarding schools of the kind founded by Hermann Lietz are still flourishing, and the group known as the Waldorf schools is growing steadily.

The first of these was started by Rudolf Steiner for children of workers at the Waldorf Astoria cigarette factory in Stuttgart in 1919. They are particularly well known for their achievements with backward and handicapped children, and consequently as a group they have tended to acquire a curative label. There are, however, some forty or so in Germany which are solely concerned with providing an alternative kind of education for normal children. They are co-educational, academically non-selective, and are able to claim that there is no financial barrier to entry.

A Steiner school education seeks to avoid one-sided emphasis on intellectual training but to take account also of the educative value of the emotions and of physical activity, both of which are considered to overlap with the domain of cognitive learning. The breadth of this approach makes it easier to bring children of all levels of academic ability together within the same class; the view is taken that to pay excessive attention to academic attainment is to make education too much concerned with training for adulthood on adult terms and too little concerned with experience which is appropriate for children at successive phases of their development as children. The curriculum comprises all the conventional subjects, but they are presented in a radically different way from the usual one and are supplemented by regular and occasional instruction in such activities as gymnastics; eurythmy, music, singing, and dancing; painting and sculpture; handicrafts of a wide variety of kinds; gardening and farming. This variety of provision and the methods used are influenced by the anthroposophical view of man's place in the totality of the universe. Religious instruction on a confessional basis is also given. In their own way the Steiner schools have continued to explore the ideas about child-centred education that were current in the 1920s and which were discussed briefly in Chapter 2.

None the less, in common with other types of private school they have in the post-war period converged with the State system to some extent. As pointed out earlier, private schools are generously subsidised and in return they must be open to inspection by the State. The teachers generally have orthodox teaching qualifications as well as, in the case of the Waldorf schools, having studied Steiner's educational principles. Of all the private schools, however, the Steiner ones have been the most critical of conventional school-leaving examinations; the twelve in Baden-Württemberg, for example, have an alternative examination which is accepted in lieu of the *Abitur*.

Another kind of alternative provision involves those who have missed the opportunity to acquire the *Abitur* during their school career. In the past the great disadvantage of the separation into the parallel tracks of the *Gymnasium*, the *Realschule*, and the *Hauptschule* was the corresponding differentiation of curricula. By this token the *Abitur* was automatically out of reach for many of those who followed the *Hauptschule* route, and though the *Aufbaugymnasium* offered some degree of compensation here there was also a need to provide opportunities to make up the leeway for those who were beyond school age. For this purpose two kinds of institution were created. The first was the evening school (*Abendgymnasium*) for those who had completed some kind of trade training and were now in employment; in this a demanding programme of at least seventeen weekly periods of instruction, spread over some three to four years, could lead to the *Abitur* and the full *Hochschulreife*. Indeed, the programme was so demanding, involving as it did the full range of subjects normally taught in the *Gymnasium*, that employers were officially requested to allow candidates a year's leave of absence during which financial assistance from the State enabled them to give adequate time to the completion of their preparation for the examination. The other opening created for those who had completed a trade training was full-time attendance at a college

(*Kolleg*) specifically for the purpose of acquiring the *Abitur*. This attend-ance, too, is subsidised by the State. During the 1960s the numbers studying at *Abendgymnasien* and *Kollegs* increased substantially.

VOCATIONAL EDUCATION

In an earlier section the traditional importance of vocational education for the German economy was discussed. The period since the war, and in particular the last decade, have seen a growing complexity in this sector which has certainly increased the range of opportunities available but, equally, has made them difficult to co-ordinate. Co-ordination rather than the creation of new institutions has therefore begun to receive the main emphasis in policy.

THE *BERUFSSCHULE*

The *Berufsschule* is the foundation of the vocational education system, providing compulsory part-time schooling between the school-leaving age and the age of 18, generally speaking a period of three years. The study is normally carried on in conjunction with an apprenticeship and as a rule involves one day's attendance per week for anything from eight to twelve periods of instruction. While the emphasis is on subject matter directly related to the trade being taken up, the curriculum also includes German, civics, and in some *Länder* religious education. Here the influence of Kerschensteiner is still in evidence in the view that the acquisition of technical knowledge and skills must not be allowed to exclude the general education of the whole personality, and in particular the inculcation of civic virtues and the development of understanding of the problems of a modern industrialised democracy.

As an illustration of the efforts that were made via the *Berufsschule* to promote understanding of the growth of the German economy in the 1950s a sample topic from the syllabus followed in one school may prove illuminating.[2]

[2] O. Monsheimer, *Drei Generationen Berufsschularbeit,* Weinheim, 1970, ed., pp. 395–401.

TOPIC: STRIKES

Aims

1. Pupils should become acquainted with the social, economic, political, and legal consequences of a strike.
2. Pupils should learn to form a personal opinion after consideration of the pros and cons of this social problem.

Teaching Aids

1. Newspaper reports and pictures from illustrated magazines dealing with the strikes in the Hamburg transport services and the Bavarian steel industry.
2. Statements of the German employers' confederation and the trade unions.
3. from *Der Spiegel* of 6.2.1954, "Expanding wages policy".
4. Chart showing productivity and wages in real terms during the period 1950–3. *Die Zeit*, No. 33.
5. Projector.
6. Books in class library.

Scheme of Instruction

I. Introduction

The following questions are asked:

1. What is the meaning of the word "strike"?
   Explanation of its derivation.
2. Why do strikes take place?
   Knauer's lexicon: in order to achieve economic and political demands.
3. Who can initiate a strike?
   The workers or the trade unions – the strike ballot.
4. Is there a right to strike?
   The justification on the part of the workers is enshrined in the constitutions of a number of *Länder* in the Federal Republic which explicitly guarantee the right to strike.
   Employers agree that in contrast to the laws of the Third Reich the strike is once more permissible but maintain that this is still far removed from "legal status".
   The opinion of the President of the Republic.

5. What course does a strike take?

The general agreement on salaries and wages between the social partners (trade unions and employers' federations) is announced.

Employers are called upon to conclude a new wage settlement.

If the negotiations are unsuccessful the union brings its members out on strike.

The strike leaders organise picketing.

Where there are disturbances the State authorities intervene — emergency services! Meanwhile negotiations between the two sides continue. A decision is taken to prolong the strike. There is recourse to the independent arbitration machinery of the State. An agreement is achieved and a new wages contract comes into being.

6. Who cannot strike?

Should doctors refuse to treat the sick?

Should dairies refuse to deliver milk for young children?

Water supplies?

II. Development of the Theme

(Socratic method.)

Basis for wage demands:

1. In the past: wages do not keep up with the standard of living.
2. Today: the gross national product should be redistributed. The worker desires greater participation in the success of the enterprise. Reduction of profits of entrepreneurs.
3. Consciously or unconsciously the employee compares his opportunities with those of the employer.
   (a) The employer has the opportunity to increase his capital in a favourable market situation or through coincidence of the market.
   (b) He, the employee, has the opportunity for bonus earnings by virtue of his own efforts or through tax reform.
   (c) In inflationary situations workers, both blue and white collar, have exerted themselves virtually in vain. The income of entrepreneurs could also dwindle through a fall in capital values.

4. *Effects*
   (a) Boom conditions as a result of the increased purchasing power of employees — or merely a redistribution?

(b) The employer is forced towards rationalisation — towards technological advance — and the price of rationalisation? — Redundancies?

(c) The level of investment falls.

III. Consequences of a Strike

(To be pursued in group work.)

1. *Social consequences*

(a) People who think and act in social terms strive for a natural and harmonious balance between self-interest and brotherly love. The term "social" means the organic collectivity of all related parts of the whole nation.

(b) The moral laws of truly social human beings are:

(i) "My" rights cease where the rights of "others" begin.

(ii) "You are another me."

(iii) "Do as you would be done by."

(c) In a real social community (democracy) the majority must always take account of the rights of the "other parts" of the whole, and the minority for its part through its feeling of shared responsibility demands for itself no greater rights than those which are also accorded to "other" parts.

(d) In consequence the inalienable right of the great majority, e.g. to public transport, to supplies of gas and water, unquestionably takes precedence over the so-called "right" to strike of a small minority which can in the end lead to a dictatorship of the minority and to chaos.

(e) In such cases the minority is ignoring the fact that it is acting unsocially towards: pensioners, refugees, those on fixed incomes, all consumers — and thereby against itself.

2. *Economic consequences*

(a) Interruptions in the development of the economy.

(i) In 1860 a wages strike affected almost exclusively the workers and management of the company. On account of the interdependability of all economic activities — divisions of labour — strikes nowadays cause disruption throughout the economic life of the nation. Example: ball-bearing production.

(ii) There is always the danger that a strike which is started by a stroke of the pen at trade union headquarters will not remain localised but may precipitate an economic catastrophe – sympathy strikes.

(b) Pay rises

(i) Rise in train and bus fares. The "victory" achieved in the name of social justice is paid for in part out of the pockets of other wage and salary earners – the strike becomes unpopular.

(ii) Price rises endanger exports which are vital for our survival – competition.

(c) Loss of earnings.

Even after taking into account strike money paid out by the unions in Bavaria, the workers only received half their normal income.

How long must they work, to make up this loss of earnings, even allowing for the now increased wages?

(i) In Hamburg every day of the strike cost the transport companies 300,000 D-Marks, which must be paid out of the public purse.

(ii) The harvest is not brought in.

(iii) Tax reforms are jeopardised – higher personnel costs require higher taxes.

3. *Political consequences*

(a) A strike deepens the gulf between the political parties.

The *SPD* leader criticises the bourgeois government, calling the strike the "bill". He points out that since the end of the war there has been no strike under a social democratic administration.

(b) Stimulus for Communism.

Slogans: "A just revolt against privately owned companies" – "courageous resistance to Adenauer's EEC policy" – the *DDR* indulges in incitement: leaflets, declarations of solidarity.

(c) In war.

Strike of munitions workers and troops in combat!

4. *Legal consequences*

(a) For the employee who belongs to a union.

(i) Summary dismissal for "breach of contract" Every worker

has the basic right to pursue his work without interruption.
Verdict of an industrial court: despite the strike call the employee has an obligation to fulfil his contract.

(ii) Summary dismissal impossible.

Verdict of another industrial court: in the event of a strike call by his union the employee has a right to strike. This right to strike ("collective right") takes precedence over duties arising out of an individual contact.

Result: the federal industrial court must finally decide this open question – Strike law?

(b) For the non-union employee.

(i) Wage entitlement.

He is prevented by pickets from going to work.

The picket – or the union, should he be acting on its instructions – becomes responsible for compensation:

of the employee for loss of wages;

of the employer for losses incurred through reduction in working time.

(ii) No wage entitlement.

The employee cannot work because there is a strike in a part of the company, e.g. the power-workers' strike.

In normal circumstances any interruption of work is basically debited to the employer.

In a situation of enforced general idleness the courts assume that the economic consequences of this interruption must be borne by all members of the "social group" – here the employees – which has initiated it.

(iii) Women who did not generally participate in the strike had to be paid by the employer although the men who do the preparatory and terminal work for them were absent.

IV Findings

1. Wage increases are not only defensible in so far "as they derive from the growth of general productivity of labour" (statement of economics research institutes). Against: Agartz, director of the economics institute of the trade union, demands wage increases irrespective of the state of productivity (expanding wages policy).

2. Professor Götz Briefe: "The trade union struggle over the share of total production that wage earners as a group should be entitled to is not a struggle against the economy but the fulfilment of a task for which there is no other agency in the capitalist system." Gerhart Hauptmann's "Wavers" – a reminder!

3. The strike weapon should only be used when all possibilities of coming to a compromise between the social partners are exhausted.

4. But it must then be used with a sense of responsibility towards the general public and guaranteeing those structures demanded by a democratic State which wishes to be civilised and under the rule of the law.

5. If the gross national product is growing through a rise in productivity price reductions are better than wage increases for they benefit all consumers.

6. A desirable partnership is made more difficult to achieve because
   (a) not all entrepreneurs have a "social conscience";
   (b) the trade unions can misuse their power. Sense of responsibility of trade union officials is high.

7. Wage increases frequently result in price rises and so on. Wage-price spiral. Endless screw. Dange of inflation. (This need not always be the case.)

8. Strikes are bad for everyone. Amicable agreement is the better solution. Recommendation: disputes over wage and salary negotiations to be settled in future by commonly agreed arbitration tribunals.

9. "Don't kill the goose that lays the golden egg."
   Newspaper report: work force of a factory in the USA decides on voluntary wage reductions in order to increase the competitiveness of their goods through price reductions and safeguard their jobs.

10. Attempted solution in Sweden: wages tied to the cost of living index. If the cost of living rises, wages also rise. The two run parallel.

11. In order to provide an incentive for genuine co-operation on the part of workers the employer must allow them to participate in the enterprise through profit sharing. That is the real meaning of partnership.

12. It shall never be forgotten that a "just wage" must be linked to "just treatment of people": security of employment, concern over

accommodation, social security in illness, emergencies and old age, a health service, acknowledgement of effort, interest in work, better working conditions, promotion opportunities, understanding and praise, advice in personal matters. The climate of the company.

V. Oral and Written Exercises

1. Has one the right to strike?
2. What means can strikers use to carry a strike through?
   Strike leaders. Pickets — propaganda. Sympathy strike. Sit-in. Sabotage.
3. What means can employers use?
   Lockouts. "Black lists." Insurance against loss of production. Relief works.
4. How is a strike ended?
   Arbitration procedures. Mandatory State arbitration.
5. How is a strike judged?

VI. Revision

With reference to officially provided information for instruction in social affairs, published by the department for home affairs of the *Land* of Hesse, September 1954.

This extract from a *Berufsschule* curriculum has been quoted at length for the wealth of insight which it offers into the aims that have permeated the mainstream of German vocational education. Its tidy schematisation illustrates the ideal of the well-structured essay. Elements of ethics, politics, and economics are skilfully blended to explain and support the capitalist system, and the anti-Communist atmosphere of the period is also apparent. It raises interesting questions regarding the relationship between moral and civic education, on the one hand, and political ideology, on the other. And there is ample scope for speculation as to how far it is designed as an opinion-forming exercise and what contribution teaching of this kind has made to Germany's record in industrial relations since the war.

THE *BERUFSGRUNDSCHULE*

However successful German technical and vocational education has been as a whole, one of its problems has always been that it forced a choice of career on many young people prematurely. For many years after the war the school-leaving age was 14 and it was calculated that no more than half of those who completed apprenticeships remained in the trade for which they were trained. Even the rise in the school-leaving age to 15 has not entirely solved the problem. For this reason there arose the idea of the *Berufsgrundschule* which provides one year of full-time education after the *Hauptschule* or the *Realschule*, with a very strong emphasis on vocational guidance. Though schools of this kind are still somewhat experimental and not always recognisable entities separate from other institutions of vocational education, they should be seen in the general context of the suggestion made in the *Strukturplan* that a pre-vocational year of this kind should be obligatory for all those who leave school at the end of the lower secondary stage. While an innovation of this kind is widely supported in educational circles it is less likely to be welcomed in the industrial companies which are responsible for the bulk of apprenticeship training. It is therefore one of the main controversies surrounding the future of technical and vocational education in the Federal Republic and, of course, relates closely to the development of *Stufenausbildung* discussed earlier. None the less, the preparation of guidelines for the curriculum in a pre-vocational year has been put in hand by the *Kultusministerkonferenz*.

THE *BERUFSAUFBAUSCHULE*

The *Berufsaufbauschule* takes vocational education beyond the level possible in the *Berufsschule* by means of full-time courses of two or three years' duration, part-time courses over six to seven years, or combinations of the two. The five groupings into which these schools divide are (a) general–industrial, (b) industrial–technical, (c) commercial, (d) domestic science–nursing–welfare, (e) agricultural. In all cases the curriculum includes compulsory German, a foreign language, history and civics, mathematics, natural sciences, to which are then added the particular subjects appropriate to the group. The important feature of the *Berufsaufbauschule* is that its terminal examination confers the *Fachschulreife*, a qualification which opens the way to certain promotions within industry or alternatively can be regarded as equivalent to the leaving certificate of the *Realschule* and hence entitles the holder to enter a *Kolleg* or one of the special types of *Gymnasium* listed earlier or, if the wish is to remain more explicitly within the vocational sector, a *Fachoberschule*.

THE *FACHOBERSCHULE*

The *Fachoberschule* is perhaps best described as the vocational and technical alternative to the general education provided in the top classes of the *Gymnasium*. It represents years 11 and 12 of full-time education. It is at present open to those holding the *mittlere Reife*, whether acquired in a *Realschule* or a *Gymnasium*, and is intended eventually to be open to all those holding the *Abitur I*, the projected lower secondary leaving certificate. Those candidates who have completed the couse at a *Berufsaufbauschule* or have both the *mittlere Reife* and a completed apprenticeship behind them may enter at the halfway stage of the course. In the first year the curriculum is made up of general education, specialised instruction, and practical training; in the second there are thirty weekly periods of instruction of which at least three-fifths are devoted to general education. The compulsory subjects within this programme are German, social studies, mathematics, natural sciences, a foreign language, and physical education. Successful completion of the course gives an entitlement to enter the specialist sector of higher education which comprises the *Fachhochschulen*. The *Fachoberschulen* are very similar to some of the specialist *Gymnasien* such as the economics and business studies, the technology or the domestic science variants; in Baden-Württemberg and Schleswig-Holstein the emphasis is on these *Gymnasien* rather than on the *Fachoberschulen*. In practice, however, there is a very comparable clientele and outcome in the two cases. The main difference is that the *Gymnasium* course is of three years' duration, that of the *Fachoberschule* only two. In this connection the *Berufsoberschule*, which is a type of school found in Baden-Württemberg and Bavaria, should also be mentioned, its function being to provide opportunities for promising young people in the vocational system to acquire the *fachgebundene Hochschulreife*.

THE *BERUFSFACHSCHULE*

The *Berufsfachschulen* make up a composite genre within which a wide range of activities are accommodated. At one end of the scale courses are provided which lead to qualifications at a comparable level to those obtained in the *Berufsschule* but which do not require a concurrent apprenticeship and can therefore be pursued full-time; at the other are courses leading to the *fachgebundene Hochschulreife*. In this latter case it would seem likely that the schools offering this kind of provision will sooner or later be subsumed within the *Fachoberschule* category. The most characteristic courses would probably be those leading to such qualifications as nursery and technical or laboratory assistants of various kinds or to middle-level commercial and clerical credentials.

THE *FACHSCHULE*

The *Fachschule* provides advanced further education for those over the age of 18; entrants must have a school-leaving certificate, sometimes at least that of the *Realschule*, an initial trade or professional qualification, and a period of experience in employment behind them. The courses are generally of from six months to two years' duration if followed full-time, two to four years part-time, and provide a specialised training for middle-level technical occupations. While these institutions have in the past been terminal, it appears likely that they will take on the alternative function of preparing their students for entry into specialist higher education, the *Fachhochschulen*. Though there are *Fachschulen* catering for a great variety of specialisms, particular emphasis has in recent years been placed on those that are primarily for the training of technicians on account of the periodic shortages of this kind of manpower that have been experienced.

In general the pace of development in the vocational education sector has been such that when analysed in detail it appears a ramshackle structure which would benefit from a thoroughgoing reorganisation. In fact the *Strukturplan* was a step in this direction, and in coming years a major rationalisation of the system would seem likely, not only to give it cohesion in itself but to make it less segregated from the general educational system. It is an increasingly obvious aim of educational policy to link the two together and thereby make possible a more balanced relationship between the educational opportunities provided and the prospects for employment that subsequently have to be faced.

CHAPTER 6

Comprehensive Schools and Curriculum Development

It was observed earlier that in the years after the war the relationship between the structure of the school system and the country's economic needs was assumed to be more or less the right one and that there was a corresponding disinclination to contemplate changes. Consequently the catalogue of types of school and the interrelationships between them which were set out in the previous chapter come across as a strongly traditional structure which the variety of experimental forms that have been appearing in recent years has not fundamentally altered. The one innovation which has yet to be described and discussed, the *Gesamtschule* (comprehensive school), is, however, of a different order, for if adopted on a widespread scale it would revolutionise the structure of German education.

As noted in Chapter 2, the idea is far from new, having been explored by various pioneers during the Weimar Republic. Then the *Einheitsschule*, as it was called, was the natural aspiration of radical reformist groups such as the *Bund entschiedener Schulreformer*. In the immediate post-war period this minority tradition was nurtured in the Soviet Zone and the 1946 Law (*Gesetz zur Demokratisierung der deutschen Schule*) was hailed as the fulfilment of these radical hopes. In the period of the "cold war", when commentary by spokesmen for the two Germanies on each other's education systems contained a fair element of mutual vilification, the very word *Einheitsschule* was anathema to those in the West.

This inevitably provided a further reinforcement of the aversion to comprehensively structured systems. And even when this violent aversion had abated somewhat and the issue of structure could be viewed more objectively, the term was still sufficiently emotionally loaded to ensure that it would not be used in the Federal Republic. In any case it had come more and more to signify not a comprehensive school but a comprehensive school system, and since the prospect of introducing such a system always seemed remote, the new term *Gesamtschule* was adopted to describe the West German comprehensive school.

A further distinction has to be made between two models, the "additive" and the "integrated" *Gesamtschule*. The additive type is a natural extension of a development that was not uncommon after 1945 whereby elementary and intermediate schools were sometimes housed in the same group of buildings, remaining separate as far as internal organisation was concerned but under the direction of a single head whose task it was to ensure that co-operation developed between the two institutions, especially with regard to such matters as transfer of pupils from one to the other. By adding the *Gymnasium* in to such an agglomeration, a multilateral type of comprehensive school was created, and for obvious reasons the expression *kooperative Gesamtschule* was used as an alternative designation. The earliest experiments were with school complexes of this kind. The integrated type, on the other hand, involves the complete removal of the tripartite structure, keeping children of the entire range of ability together in the same institution throughout the period of compulsory schooling.

THE DEBATE OVER THE *GESAMTSCHULE*

The debate over the *Gesamtschule* gained momentum from the publication by the *Deutscher Bildungsrat* in 1969 of a special study on the subject of the setting up of experiments of this kind (*Einrichtung von Schulversuchen mit Gesamtschulen*). This study reflects the hopes that were entertained for comprehensive schools in the later 1960s:

"the starting point for all justifications for the need for *Gesamtschulen* lies in the demand for equality of opportunity. Furthermore it is nowadays becoming clear that educational reform in the cause of greater equality of opportunity can also lead to better schools for all pupils; it can enhance the achievement of the education system as a whole, contribute to a greater individualisation of learning, and come to terms with the fact that in our society all people are increasingly oriented towards an academic education."[1]

[1] *Deutscher Bildungsrat, Einrichtung von Schulversuchen mit Gesamtschulen,* Bonn, 1969, p. 21.

The general case has thus followed a pattern that has been familiar elsewhere.

The primary argument has been the need to change a situation in which the great majority of children were effectively denied access to an academic type of education. The *Gesamtschule* provides the most obvious framework within which a commonality of general objectives can be pursued for the entire school population throughout the period of compulsory attendance. It must appear surprising that it has taken so long for this idea to be taken seriously and advanced as a practical policy objective. There are, however, very clear reasons for the reluctance to abandon the tripartite system. German education, particularly as provided in the *Gymnasium* and the *Realschule*, has traditionally been permeated by the notion of achievement (*Leistung*); the critics of the *Gesamtschule* have constantly maintained that there are very large qualitative differences in the education required for the more and the less academically gifted and that to put them together in the same school must mean that, on the one hand, excessive demands are made on the less able while those with a natural inclination towards academic work are insufficiently stretched; thereby, it is claimed, both groups become frustrated and justice is done to neither.

As a result of this concern for *Leistung* the response to the increasing demand for education in the post-war period has been to expand provision of the existing types of school. Thus where formerly the *Gymnasium* tended to be accessible largely to those living in or near urban areas, the network has in recent years spread to the less-populous regions. Not only has there been this improvement in the distribution of *Gymnasien* throughout the Federal Republic but the numbers of such schools have also greatly increased even in districts which previously were comparatively well provided for, and in a much greater variety of forms than before, as was noted in the previous chapter. Probably more significant has been the expansion of the *Realschule* sector. It has already been observed that the more intensely academic education of the *Gymnasium* has been unattractive to many parents who have, on the other hand, regarded the *Realschule* as a more realistic means to advancement for their children. Consequently the reluctance to abandon the tripartite system can further be explained by the view that with the expansion of provision that has already taken place and with the new flexible admissions procedures which recognise the principle of parental choice, a *Gymnasium* or *Realschule* education is available to all those who desire it and that the defence of the achievement principle is not at the expense of a democratisation of the system.

The advocates of the *Gesamtschule* while accepting that the scope for differentiation within the existing system has been greatly increased in recent years none the less maintain that the segregation into different types of school reduces the possibilities for adapting education to the needs of the individual pupil. This reflects a reaction against the standard practice in the traditional system whereby each class stayed together for all subjects throughout its progress through the school. German schools had always set great store by the continuity that this guaranteed, and it was generally thought that it fostered a drive towards achievement in the entire range of subjects and not merely those to which individual pupils felt particularly attracted. The argument in favour of the *Gesamtschule* is, therefore, that it makes possible a system in which the common elements in the curriculum can be reduced to a "core" and that this can be supplemented by various courses in which there would be grouping according to ability and inclination. The aim is a flexibility such as to allow individual pupils to proceed at their own pace and build up their curriculum partly on a *table d'hôte,* partly on an *à la carte* basis. A school-counselling service is generally advocated as a necessary addition to help pupils make choices appropriate to their abilities and aptitudes.

It is the question of appropriateness that is the main bone of contention. The traditionalists begin from the more stern assumption that a good many pupils would be inclined to make the choices that were particularly attractive to them at a given time, that they would shy away from contact with anything that departed from the line of least resistance, and that consequently their education would be built up in accordance not with serious epistemological principles but with the haphazard dictates of individual caprice. For a rounded education, it is maintained, a minimum of knowledge is required in all subjects, and this broad basis would be jeopardised in the highly differentiated provision that is proposed within the *Gesamtschule.*

The contrary argument is that a differentiation based on individual choices would capitalise on the pupil's motivation in subjects where a particular aptitude is shown and would reduce apathy in those where there is an absence of motivation. It is further pointed out that this approach would greatly reduce the problem of grade-repeating which, it is claimed, tends to cause over-burdening of pupils, frustration, and early leaving. Here the discussion has markedly sociological overtones: a good deal is made of the dependence of school achievement on social background, and the hypothesis is put forward that this dependence is especially strong in linguistic and literary subjects, less strong in mathematics, and still less strong in natural sciences.[2] Now it is well established that the traditional *Gymnasium* curriculum and even that of the *Realschule* have a literary and linguistic bias. Consequently it is argued that a greater measure of specialisation would be to the benefit of pupils from working-class backgrounds; they would not be so hampered by cultural disadvantages and their motivation would be greatly reinforced by their progress in individual subjects.

It is obvious that a debate of this kind has little meaning until the specific content of the curriculum is discussed and until there is some evidence regarding what is and is not possible within a *Gesamtschule* structure. For this reason the idea has remained at the experimental stage in the majority of *Länder*, reflecting a caution about innovation that has characterised attitudes to education in the Federal Republic throughout the post-war period. Consequently the *Bildungsrat* has spelt out as specific research objectives the need to discover to what extent the *Gesamtschule* could succeed in offering to pupils of all levels of ability an academic education adequate for their stage of development; to what extent young people are in a position to make their own choices in a responsible way; and whether freedom of choice of this kind would really be in danger of leading to diffuse and unsystematic learning.

The pedagogical discussion and the question of the evaluation of the experiments with *Gesamtschulen* has in general been overshadowed by the ideological polarisation over the issue. The radical case is that the hierarchically structured school system mirrors the class structure of society and thereby tends to preserve social inequalities. The selective process is viewed as a kind of programming of individuals to a specific level of education and hence of status in life, a "self-fulfilling prophecy" whereby individuals tend to perform in accordance with what is expected of them, however erroneous the foundation for those expectations may be. The

[2] *Deutscher Bildungsrat, op. cit.,* p. 26.

Gesamtschule is seen as a means of breaking up existing social structures by fostering awareness of social class divisions:

"Common social experience in the *Gesamtschule* should not aim at accommodation to harmony in the community. The meeting of the various social classes in the common school can rather lead to the discovery and awareness of social differences. Social conflicts can be articulated and collectively discussed. The pupils come to understand that the forms of life that are taken for granted in the family are not in the nature of things and unchangeable. The perspective which can thus be gained *vis-à-vis* one's own social origin and the forms of life that have previously been taken for granted can operate in an individual's favour."[3]

The conservative case is that the aim of equality of opportunity is better served by more generous provision of the existing types of school, and those in favour of radical change do accept that the growth of the network of *Gymnasien* and *Realschulen* has brought a more equitable represent-ation of the various social groups into the early classes of these schools. But the fact that a higher proportion of working-class pupils tend to leave the *Gymnasium* early, generally in order to transfer to vocational education, is considered a failure on its part, a criticism of the general education which it aims to provide. The assumption is that more of these young people would remain in conventional full-time education if a system of *Gesamtschulen* were introduced and thereby break down the relative social homogeneity that has survived at the upper secondary stage. The conservatives maintain, on the other hand, that to promote social equality in schools at all costs would be to destroy the sense of purpose of the system which has always been the achievement of the highest standards of which individual pupils are capable.

Thus the social argument becomes enmeshed with the pedagogical one regarding the extent to which the respective systems can succeed in getting the best out of the pupils entrusted to them. Here the possibilities for constructive research in the form of comparative study of the two systems are considerable, for the supporters of the *Gesamtschule* do tend to maintain that under the kind of reorganisation which they advocate, the

[3] *Ibid.*, p. 30.

principle of *Leistung* and the sense of individual challenge associated with it are preserved, if not indeed enhanced.

In this connection an odd feature of the debate has been the tendency to neglect consideration of the role of the teachers. Arguments about differentiation and integration are rehearsed under the assumption that the commitment of the teaching staff to their work is constant in all types of school. Yet it is obvious, firstly, that the interest and energy of individual teachers can vary enormously, and, secondly, that this variation can be seriously affected by their attitudes to the schools in which they are employed. To judge by the official statements of the associations of teachers in *Gymnasien* and *Realschulen*, the opposition to the *Gesamtschule* idea in these sectors of the teaching profession has been implacable, but it is always difficult to be certain to what degree such statements really reflect the views of the rank and file membership.

This kind of opposition has been evident in Hesse, the *Land* which has had the most ambitious plans for a reorganisation. The intermediate and secondary teachers have been supported by parents' associations, by the chambers of industry and commerce, and by the representatives of the smallest administrative districts, the communes (*Gemeinden*). The opposition of the latter reflected the political decision whereby the control which they had traditionally exercised over their own local schools was transferred to the larger administrative units (*Kreise*), a level at which it was easier to push through the reorganisation by dint of political and economic pressures.[4] These few indications are sufficient to illustrate the strength of feeling that the *Gesamtschule* controversy has aroused even in the fairly radical *Land* of Hesse where the Social Democrats have generally been the governing party. It goes without saying that the issue touches on deeply held and locally rooted beliefs about education, and it would be naive not to regard the involvement of teachers as a factor that is likely to have an important bearing on the success of an innovation. Yet it must be said that research in this field shows a tendency to dismiss the opposition of teachers as mindless resistance to change and to stop short of analysing their fears.

---

[4] CERI (Centre for Educational Research and Innovation), *Case Studies of Educational Innovation II*, OECD, Paris, 1974, p. 192.

These centre on the problems of motivation and achievement, not so much in the *Oberstufe* where the "core and course" principle is accepted and is to be implemented throughout the Federal Republic by the school year 1976/7, but in the first six years of the *Gesamtschule*, years 5–10 of school attendance. It is therefore interesting to examine the proposals of the *Bildungsrat* regarding curriculum and grouping during this period, also known as the *Mittelstufe* of the system.[5]

GUIDELINES FOR THE CURRICULUM

The ideas on a syllabus for German are strongly influenced by recently popularised theories about the relationship between social class and linguistic development. The way in which the mother tongue is taught is seen as a means towards the reduction of social inequalities. Much greater importance is attached to oral communication than in the past, and it is suggested that classes in literature should also be oriented towards the development of this skill. The variety of idiom that results from the mixing of the social classes in the *Gesamtschule* is regarded as stimulating and beneficial, and it is recommended that, apart from special remedial courses, there should as a rule be no grouping according to ability or inclination before the seventh school year. The main form of differentiation suggested for the later years of the *Gesamtschule* is by way of supplementary courses. These are especially apposite for instruction in literature but are also suggested for the sphere of language where the possibility of interdisciplinary work linking the mother tongue with mathematics or foreign-language instruction has been mooted.

In foreign languages the emphasis is also on communication and an exposure to a wider variety of registers than has been usual in the past. A common-core syllabus is envisaged aimed primarily at developing oral–aural skill. Unlike the mother tongue, however, it is thought that foreign-language courses should be begun at various stages, for some immediately on entry to the *Gesamtschule*, and perhaps as late as the age of 14 or 16 for others, using whatever methods are most appropriate to the stage of development of the pupil and pursued in correspondingly varying degrees of intensiveness. It is suggested that the loss of interest brought about by continuous study of a subject over a number of years is particularly severe

[5] *Deutscher Bildungsrat, op. cit.,* pp. 54–62.

in foreign languages, and experiments with "crash" and "refresher" courses are advocated. Through this variety of approach it is hoped that the need for grouping by ability will be greatly reduced and certainly not practised during the first year. The advent of the *Gesamtschule* is also expected to broaden the range of languages offered, with Russian available in all schools and Greek no longer confined to the dwindling number of classical *Gymnasien*. Finally, much stress is laid on the precision required in devising foreign-language courses, relating content and methods to clearly defined aims.

The deliberations over the place of history in the curriculum start from an assumption that during the first few years of the *Gesamtschule* pupils can gain only a very slight understanding of the nature of the discipline as conveyed by concepts of interdependence and development or the relationship between continuity and change. For this reason it is recommended that for the first one or two years there should be a preparatory course of general history giving some idea of its anthropological basis, the determinants of action, and the scope for decision in human affairs. Not until the eighth school year is it thought desirable to devote a larger allocation of time to history. This change in its timing within the curriculum is seen as necessitating a new approach to the teaching of history, one that combines factual learning with an understanding of theoretical models. Thus the desire is to work out a new relationship between history and social studies, uniting the two in a thematic approach and entrusting them jointly to the same teacher or to a team of teachers. A common syllabus is recommended with grouping beginning at the earliest in the fifth year of the *Gesamtschule* either into elementary and intensive courses or on the basis of areas of interest.

In the field of social studies itself the aim is, especially in the early years, to relate the instruction as far as possible to the child's direct experience; in particular, social structures and patterns of individual behaviour within the school are expected to provide themes within which concepts of role, group, and so on can be developed – a further important task is to develop the ability to seek out information independently and to evaluate it critically. With this goes instruction in such methods as enable the pupil not only to handle factual knowledge when working alone but also to support an argument in group discussion. In general, grouping by ability is not favoured in social studies, heterogeneity of classes being considered advantageous for the study of social structures and patterns of behaviour. But an indication is given of the opportunities for differentiation within classes and for supplementary courses for those with a particularly keen interest towards the end of *Mittelstufe* period.

"Arbeitslehre", a composite intended as a preparation for working life, was originally thought of as a subject for the *Hauptschule* only, but the aim is to develop it as an element in the curriculum for all pupils in the *Gesamtschule*. An induction into the technical, economic, and social aspects of the modern labour market is not provided elsewhere and is considered essential for all pupils including those going on to upper secondary and higher education. This aim is not to be achieved exclusively through *Arbeitslehre,* for many other subjects such as natural sciences, social studies, and mathematics have a contribution to make. Consequently there is some uncertainty still as to what the subject *Arbeitslehre* itself comprehends. The *Bildungsrat* suggests experimental work along four specific lines: first, in co-operation with natural sciences, an introduction should be given to elementary technologies, technical thinking, and experimental activity through construction of models and individual projects; second, in collaboration with social sciences the aim is to find ways of imparting insights into economic relationships; third, group activity among pupils is to be fostered which should in turn encourage the development of the project method in other subjects; fourth, experiments are considered necessary to discover how far work experience is beneficial for pupils in their ninth and tenth school years and how feasible is its organisation. No hard and fast rules are suggested for the stage at which differentiation in *Arbeitslehre* should begin, but it is categorically stated that segregation with a view to the award of different types of qualification should not take place before the tenth school year. At this point it is considered appropriate to introduce supplementary courses geared to the requirements of particular trades and elementary polytechnical training in such fields as electrical or chemical engineering.

The starting point for consideration of the mathematics syllabus is the universal requirement in modern society to understand "mathematicised" information. The problem is seen therefore as being as much to develop this kind of understanding as to teach mathematics *per se*; the procedures involved are to be made comprehensible to the layman. Mathematics requires earlier differentiation than other subjects, but there are misgivings about effecting this exclusively through grouping by ability. Experiments in differentiation based on content and methods are considered desirable so that a variety of ways towards mathematical understanding can be explored.

The natural sciences syllabus is to begin in the first year of the *Gesamtschule*, since children in this age group show a great interest in observing, describing, and experimenting with natural phenomena, and have the ability to perceive elementary causal relationships. It is pointed out that particular care must be taken to gear the teaching to this stage of development by laying stress on description and elementary experiments. It is therefore considered best to provide a general science course in the first two years of the *Gesamtschule*, on the one hand, because all aspects of science must be taken into account, and, on the other, because specialised teaching in physics, chemistry, and biology would lead to an over-burdening of the pupils; the discrepancy between the instruction given at the primary level and strongly discipline-oriented teaching at the beginning of the *Gesamtschule* could be very great. General science can begin from a biological perspective and then analyse the phenomena observed by children from physical and chemical standpoints. At the same early stage it is suggested that elementary technology should be introduced. The idea of team teaching is put forward as being appropriate for work in general science in the early years. After the next stage of specialised teaching some return to interdisciplinary work based in particular on anthropological themes is advocated, perhaps in the last two years of the *Mittelstufe*. At this point, too, some differentiation into elementary and intensive courses is considered advisable.

These, then, are the general guidelines that were provided at federal level for those who over the past few years have been attempting to pioneer new approaches to the curriculum in *Gesamtschulen*. In Hesse, for example, where in 1972/3 there were eighty-four such schools, specialist working parties of teachers and researchers have been preparing new syllabuses for the *Mittelstufe*. This work has reflected the familiar tension between somewhat grandiose plans to elaborate an all-embracing taxonomy of curricular objectives and the more down-to-earth require-ment to put on paper the specific details about content that are necessary to win the interest and respect of practising teachers. The hope has been that the changes in the curriculum would not in fact be confined to the

Gesamtschulen but that the new syllabuses could eventually become operative throughout the normal school system. This aspiration has, however, revealed the magnitude of the task of involving teachers on a widespread scale in what is termed the "concretisation" of guidelines. It is clear that unless the teachers themselves are sufficiently interested to take part in the process of working out the practical "concrete" details of what is to happen in the classroom, the innovations that are advocated are likely to remain a dead letter.

This has led the *Bildungsrat* to consider ways of promoting practice-oriented curriculum development. Recommendations published in 1973 (*Zur Förderung praxisnaher Curriculum – Entwicklung*) suggested as a means to this end the setting up of regional centres rather along the lines of the teachers' centres in the United Kingdom. According to the plan a centre would be set up to serve a region of about a million inhabitants strategically placed for convenience of access from all schools. Where previously curriculum work had been unco-ordinated and suffered from lack of funds, it was now thought that the new institutionalisation of the process – fifteen centres with about fifty full-time staff in the first four years, increasing eventually to about sixty centres – would put it on a firm footing, ensuring that it could reach out to the entire teaching profession.

Here, however, a further problem has presented itself, one that is more fundamental than the mechanics of setting up efficacious curriculum workshops, namely the interpretation of the aims of curricular change and the extent to which they coincide with the more general aim of changing society. It will be recalled that the *Bildungsrat* guidelines declared that social conflict should be brought into the centre of classroom activity. To give precision to this somewhat vague formulation is to step on to the dangerous terrain of cultural values, and a violent controversy was set in motion by the publication of the now notorious guidelines for the teaching of German and social studies in the schools of Hesse. These guidelines were accused of undermining traditional cultural values via the teaching of German language and literature and of introducing the kind of political indoctrination associated with totalitarian states via the proposals for the teaching of social studies. Teachers' and parents' associations were prominent among those protesting against the proposed "red denominational schools", as one headline dubbed them. The storm blew itself out in several marathon television debates, and the guidelines are being revised by a team less markedly dedicated to the propagation of socialist principles. The significance, however, goes beyond that of a transitory *cause célèbre*, for it underlines the difficulties involved in promoting curricular changes that have a genuine prospect of being acceptable to the teaching profession as a whole; the somewhat ham-fisted initiative in Hesse has provided a useful reminder of the importance of maturity of judgement in these matters.

The Hesse plans reflect some of the frustration at the failure of education to compensate for inequalities in society. With many children substantially hampered in their school achievement by unfavourable home background, the *Gesamtschule* has tended to be regarded as the most prominent panacea for this unsatisfactory state of affairs. Yet the implementation of comprehensive principles has in fact made little difference. An inquiry in Hesse into the effects of bringing in the *Förderstufe*, the comprehensive orientation stage designed to postpone transfer to the *Gymnasium* and thus make it less difficult for working-class children, showed that only a 2 per cent increase in such transfers was effected.[6] Thus as far as correcting the imbalance in the representation of the various social classes is concerned, the postponement of selection has by itself been largely irrelevant. Some reformist groups have seen this merely as proof that the fundamental nature of educational aims needs to be changed; and as has been seen in the case of Hesse this results in a bitter divisiveness.

A more constructive strategy has been the coupling of a *Gesamtschule* idea with that of the whole-day school (*Ganztagsschule*). It was pointed out in earlier chapters that in German schools teaching has traditionally been confined to the mornings and that children are expected to do their homework in the afternoons under the supervision of parents and grandparents whose competence and interest thus become important factors in their confidence and success. Clearly whole-day schooling could do a great deal to reduce the inequalities inherent in this situation and the *Bildungsrat* recommended an extensive introduction of *Ganztagsschulen*. While this is possible in the traditional types of school, and, indeed, is practised in a few of the newer *Gymnasien* and *Realschulen*, it may well have a better prospect of becoming widely established in the context of the *Gesamtschule*. If this were to be the case the *Gesamtschule* could then

[6] CERI, *op. cit.*, p. 183.

claim to be the agent of a transformation in the ethos of German schools. Such a leavening process is, however, still at a very early stage, and the demands that it makes on a teaching profession unaccustomed to such a level of commitment should not be underestimated.

CHAPTER 7

Higher Education

It is in higher education that the most disruptive effects of educational expansion have been felt in the Federal Republic in recent years. The painless progression from school to university, whereby possession of the *Abitur* was a guarantee of a place in any faculty of any university of the candidate's choice, has given way to recurrent crises over admissions procedures. To the dismay of school-leavers with aspirations to university study the notion of a *numerus clausus* – a fixed maximum number of students to which a faculty can restrict its intake – has spread inexorably throughout the higher education system.

In the early stages of the enforcement of these restrictions towards the end of the 1960s they were constantly declared to be acceptable only on a temporary basis. But as the problem became more and more acute, so the general dissatisfaction grew, and the issue was even taken to the Federal Constitutional Court which declared that new criteria for university entrance needed to be established which would be uniform throughout the Federal Republic. Underlying this declaration too, however, was the assumption that the phenomenon was temporary, that it was a matter of ensuring fair competition for places until the system could recover from the shock of sudden expansion. Once this difficult period was over, it was implied, there would be places at the universities for all those qualified to take them up. The temporary situation, however, has shown every indication of becoming a lasting one. Despite optimistic statements by officials and by education ministers there is growing acceptance of the fact that many of those leaving school with the *Abitur* will be denied what they regard as their right to a university place.

The resulting disillusionment is particularly severe because this is the generation that was so assiduously wooed by educational publicity in the later 1960s when the urge to double the numbers acquiring the *Abitur* became such a salient feature of educational policy. There are broadly speaking two ways of diagnosing the problem. On the one hand, there are those who regard the expansion at the upper secondary level as having been artificially stimulated without any regard for the consequences in terms of employment prospects and who now point to the fulfilment of their prophecy that an "academic proletariat" would be created, its members highly educated, but with no scope to make use of the qualifications they had obtained. On the other hand, there is the school of thought which continues to adhere to the principle of expansion and blames the crisis on the failure of higher education to expand at a corresponding rate. According to this view the absolute value to the individual of an extended education is more important than the extent to which it does or does not guarantee employment of the kind hitherto regarded as commensurate with it. Whichever explanation is accepted there remains a chronic problem of capacity.

An awareness that the problems could be anticipated and that there was therefore a need to review the provision of higher education on a federal basis can be traced back to the formation in 1957 of the *Wissenschaftsrat,* an advisory council for education and science made up of academics and prominent personalities in other spheres interested in policy for higher education. Its first major recommendation produced in 1960 (*Empfehlungen zum Ausbau der wissenschaftlichen Einrichtungen*) recognised the shortage of capacity to meet both the private demand for higher education that would result from an increase in the number of *Abiturienten* and the national economic needs in terms of qualified manpower. This publication gave the impetus for the foundation of new universities such as Bochum, Konstanz, and Bielefeld, and thereby set the process of expansion in motion. As well as new buildings, it required a swift and large-scale recruitment of university teachers. In a very short time there was a tremendous increase in the junior teaching staff, the *Mittelbau,* which rapidly became one of the most significant factors in the state of unrest into which the universities were plunged in the later 1960s.

Before the expansion of the *Mittelbau* the oligarchical structure of university government had scarcely been challenged. Executive power was effectively in the hands of the professors, for even if other groups in the university were represented in the senate or on faculty committees they did not as a rule have voting rights but merely fulfilled an advisory function. Appointment to a chair was restricted to those who, after obtaining a doctorate for original research, had passed the further exacting test of the *venia legendi* or *Habilitation*, generally speaking by submitting a higher-level dissertation. This intensively selective process had always been seen as essential in a system where the doctorate itself is relatively common, being one of two main ways of graduating from university.

The first of these two ways was the *Staatsexamen*, the obligatory route for future *Gymnasium* teachers and lawyers. This consisted of a lengthy written examination in two subjects followed by a demanding oral examination conducted by a professor of the university and a civil servant representing the tutelary ministry. Thus the State conferred on successful candidates the basic right to practise law or to teach at *Gymnasium* level, a right which was then confirmed at the end of a period of probation. In the case of *Gymnasium* teaching this lasted for two years, nowadays generally rather less, during which time candidates gave a limited amount of instruction under the supervision of experienced teachers in schools and were also required to attend method seminars and to study the theory of education. Apart, of course, from those following specifically vocational courses as, for example, in medicine, dentistry or engineering, the other form of graduation was via the *Doktorprüfung* which entailed the presentation of an original thesis and generally speaking also a written examination in one or two subsidiary subjects. While the pattern of the *Staatsexamen* has remained substantially unchanged the alternative route via the doctorate has proved too arduous for the greatly increased numbers of students entering universities in recent years. The result has been a gradual growth in the number of diplomas awarded and in the creation of the new level of *Magisterprüfung* corresponding roughly to the master's degree in the United Kingdom and the United States.

The recruitment of teaching staff to expand the *Mittelbau* had to be from the ranks of those who had either obtained or were promising candidates for the doctorate. But the *Habilitation* remained a prerequisite for appointment to a permanent post either as professor or as university lecturer. The assistants who made up the *Mittelbau* were appointed for a period of four to six years only, at the end of which time they were obliged to seek a new post with no guarantee of being able to remain in university teaching. Thus although the expansion of the *Mittelbau* provided a speedy short-term solution to the problem of finding a teaching force to cope with the growing numbers of students, it created the long-term problem of a large and potentially dissident group, many of whom, while officially forming part of the staff of the university, found that their sympathies in internal political controversies lay much more with the students than with their senior colleagues.

Clearly, then, the higher education sector in the Federal Republic is being subjected to quite new pressures, and the rate of change has accelerated accordingly. The nature of this change can only be fully understood in relation to the traditions of German higher education. At the very heart of the idea of the German university has been the notion of academic freedom as conceived by Wilhelm von Humboldt, a figure whose importance for the history of higher learning matches his impact on the *Gymnasium*. While this freedom is legally enshrined in such matters as the right to order the relationship between teaching and research, to confer degrees, and to nominate candidates for teaching appointments, its successful operation in practice depends a good deal on considerations that are less easily codified. A freedom which allows the personnel of a university to pursue their own academic interests needs to be reconciled with an unwritten obligation to display a sense of responsibility to society at large, to take particular account of national employment needs, and to be tempered with concern for the welfare of students. The pressures of the 1960s brought with them a rising tide of allegations that the universities of the Federal Republic were defaulting on these obligations.

Whatever the truth of the allegations, e.g. that the professors were "specialist idiots" (*Fachidioten*), the troubles gathered such momentum that attempts to rectify the shortcomings could only be piecemeal and have in fact led to a state of confusion. Some universities have reorganised their departmental structure, others have not; some have tried to reshape their courses and degrees in accordance with the subsequent vocational requirements of their students, others have not; at some the *Habilitation* has ceased to be a prerequisite for appointment to a post with tenure, at others it has survived. While it is a commonplace to observe that the traditional university of Humboldt is dead, it is observed with equal frequency that there is no clear concept to take its place. This disorientation has led the general public to look to the proposed new Higher Education Law, the *Hochschulrahmengesetz,* to make sense of the hotchpotch of conflicting attitudes and practices.

Before viewing the prospects of the *Hochschulrahmengesetz* as a panacea, however, it is appropriate to examine what the major sectors of higher education have stood for in the past, how they have reacted to the recent pressure of events, and in what way, if any, they could fit into a new all-embracing system.

THE "TRADITIONAL" UNIVERSITIES

Humboldt's rejuvenation of the traditional universities in the early nineteenth century suggests that he was responsible for arresting their decline. It is true that around 1700 their reputation stood very low and that many leading figures in intellectual life showed no desire to be associated with them. In the course of the eighteenth century, however, there was something of a revival, pioneered in the newer foundations of Halle, Göttingen, and Erlangen. At these universities the questioning spirit of the Enlightenment flourished, they were cradles of modern scientific research. Classical studies, too, were given fresh life by a new emphasis on the aesthetic qualities of ancient literature, a new interest in criticism. Humboldt had experienced the burgeoning spirit of inquiry at first hand as a student at Göttingen, and it became his concern to disseminate and perpetuate it throughout the network of German universities. This intent is epitomised by his creation in 1810 of the university of Berlin which was to become the model for the modern German university. It was fundamental to the life of this institution that it should be regarded as existing primarily for the purpose of academic research, and its professors were appointed on the basis of their ability and energy in the pursuit of new knowledge. It was assumed that men of such calibre would also be good teachers, for teaching was no longer to be conceived of as involving the transmission of an encyclopedia of accepted dogma but rather as a grounding in first principles and an induction into the techniques of inquiry based on those principles.

This view of higher education stands in marked contrast to the conception which underlay the reorganisation in France under Napoleon, whose objective was to turn out skilled practitioners trained to fulfil specific roles in the administration, and to this end instructed along lines laid down by the State. This contrast, moreover, illuminates an accusation that has in recent years been increasingly directed at Humboldt's conception. This is that it had the effect of divorcing the activities of the universities from the life of the nation as a whole, imbuing those involved in "academic" education with a disdain for vocational matters and thereby fostering elitism, while failing to meet the obligation to furnish the State with the kind of highly trained manpower it needed. It was, however, Humboldt's belief that the State would be best served if it was led by men of scholarship. This was in harmony with the growing conviction at the time that the German nation would rise to great heights by virtue of its superior civilisation. It was not the denial of the obligations of the university as regards useful training but rather the *interpretation* of them that gave Humboldt's dispensation its individual imprint. That this interpretation was to prove less apposite in a later era of industrialisation was no fault of Humboldt's.

So impressive was Humboldt's personality, however, so powerful his influence, that no real redefinition of the role of the traditional university in relation to society at large was subsequently considered necessary. The German universities continued to give the kind of priority to academic research that he had envisaged for them and to order their activities accordingly. The only interlude which brought a curtailment of their academic freedom came with the Third Reich. Totalitarian regimes do not as a rule tolerate apolitical scholarship, and the Nazis insisted that the activities of the universities must be pursued in accordance with the official political principles and aims. Those who had been elected to high office in them by their colleagues were, if unsympathetic to Nazi dogma, replaced by appointees of the government of the Third Reich. Voiced disapproval of this situation of creeping State stranglehold was rare; for a great many German academics at that time discretion was, in the well-worn phrase, the better part of valour. After the war it is hardly surprising that the German university community readopted gratefully and with alacrity the Humboldt principle of academic freedom.

The particular conditions under which this freedom has existed in post-war Germany has, however, made for pressures on the system as conceived by Humboldt and for growing discord among those within it. In the first place it has been a freedom circumscribed by financial stringency.

It was in line with the cultural autonomy of the *Länder* that the universities should come under their purview, but the upkeep of such costly institutions was an immense drain on resources. It was seldom that the *Land* authorities were able to meet what the universities considered to be their requirements. On the university side therefore there was some resentment at the limitations on their activities resulting from their lack of financial elbow room. This appeared only to serve to promote obduracy in the defence of those freedoms which the professors did enjoy, namely to pursue their own academic interests unhindered by excessive teaching duties. If the expenditure was considered inadequate by the universities it none the less constituted an enormous item in *Land* budgets so that on the political side there was increasing concern to get value for money in the shape of more efficient teaching. Yet precisely the opposite effect was being brought about by the tension between the two sides. For by taking refuge behind their statutory rights and duties the professors ensured a deterioration in the conditions under which students worked.

The particular dimension of academic freedom that has made German universities different from their English and American counterparts has been the so-called *Lern- und Lehrfeiheit* — freedom of learning and teaching. This idea not only granted teachers the right to teach what they wanted, but also conferred extensive freedoms on students. In the first place, once they had obtained the *Abitur* at the *Gymnasium* they had the right to enter any faculty of any university. Secondly, there was no obligation on them to complete their studies within a prescribed time; examinations were taken when they considered themselves ready for them and dilatoriness was not discouraged. Thirdly, it was possible to move about from one university to another in order to change teachers or follow those who themselves moved. It can readily be seen that in the intimate circumstances of university life in the nineteenth century such a system had substantial advantages.

In more recent times, when the pressure of numbers has been growing, it has been less appropriate. Those students who came from the better-off families could afford to dally and postpone the moment of truth in the examination room for as long as it suited them. They could change universities to satisfy caprice, the German student could be ubiquitous as well as eternal. And the more the universities became clogged with procrastinators the more their efficiency was impaired. This vicious circle was exacerbated

by the growth of the enrolment rate which increased the administrative
burden of the professors and thereby impaired still further their effectiveness in teaching. For a long time the situation remained viable by virtue of
the fact that very meagre resources were made available to support
students from less-well-off homes. But this shortcoming in social provision
eventually came in for sharp criticism, and as it began to be cured through
increased availability of financial support, the result was an even greater
overcrowding of institutions that were already losing their effectiveness.

The other side of the problem lay, of course, in the pattern of staffing.
The powerful position of the professors continued to reflect the conditions of an earlier age. The academic who was cast in the Humboldt
mould was something of a polymath and certainly able to command the
entire field within his own discipline. But the vast advances in knowledge
and the growing tendency towards specialisation that accompanied them
made this view outdated. In the natural sciences in particular the major
centres of research came more and more to be outside the universities. The
professors ceased to be quite the imposing figures they once were. They
retained, however, a level of authority consonant with their earlier pre-
eminence and as pointed out earlier, it is frequently alleged that their new
professional vulnerability made them cling all the more firmly to their
authoritarian privileges. Whatever the truth of the allegation it is clear that
public attention was directed more and more to the hierarchical principles
of staffing in the universities. This crystallised above all when the expansion in numbers of entrants forced the corresponding recruitment of
university teachers of non-professorial rank mentioned earlier. To
reiterate, this group of assistants which lacked security of tenure and for
which career prospects were at best very loosely defined felt hard done
by, and many of its members shared the disillusionment and feeling of
neglect experienced by the students. When the steep rise in political
activism came in the 1960s it was particularly in evidence in Germany in
the demands for a more democratic structure to modify the omnipotence
of the professors.

The campaign was for decision-making to be based on the principle of
Drittelparität – equal representation of professors, assistants, and
students. But where modifications in the authority structure were made
they led to still more laborious decision-making and administrative procedures rather than to the re-establishment of the universities as effective

institutions for research and teaching. The demands for *Drittelparität* were a parallel to similar developments in the direction of co-determination in other sectors of the economy. Where they filtered through into the legislative plans of the *Länder* it was generally in the context of proposals for the comprehensive reorganisation of higher education, and in so doing they aroused fierce controversy. In Lower Saxony a group of professors went so far as to take the matter to the Federal Constitutional Court. Their claim was that the granting of extensive rights of co-determination was an infringement of the article of the Constitution which guarantees freedom of research and teaching. The point at issue was that whereas academic decisions had previously been the sole prerogative of the professors, under the principle of co-determination these decisions could lie in the hands of those insufficiently qualified to exercise such a responsibility. The Court's decision recognised the superior status of the professors by declaring that they should have 50 per cent of the votes on the faculty and subject area committees which decided on vital questions affecting teaching and research, and thereby ensured that effective control over university affairs remained in their hands.

THE TECHNOLOGICAL UNIVERSITIES

It has already been pointed out that Humboldt's conception of the university was not adequate to meet the demands of growing industrialisation in the nineteenth century. As Germany's progress in this respect accelerated so did the progress of those institutions which were not primarily concerned with the loftier ideals of scholarship but with the training of experts to do specific jobs. In the eighteenth century there had been schools for skilled craftsmen of various kinds; by the late nineteenth century they had evolved into technological universities (*Technische Hochschulen*). These new institutions thrived in the atmosphere of accelerating industrial development in the late nineteenth century, a phase when the internal combustion engine was of great importance, when chemicals, precision instruments, electricity, and steel were numbered among the key industries; and the view was taken in Germany that success in these fields depended upon systematically trained, skilled manpower. This view was and still is characterised by the high value that is placed on sound theoretical study and the employment of experts to produce more experts.

The growth of higher technical education in Germany is well illustrated by the case of the university of Karlsruhe. Its origins go back to 1825 when two institutions were merged to form a *"Polytechnische Schule"*. One of these was an architectural college-cum-civil engineering institute which had been built up by the architect Friedrich Weinbrenner. The other was the engineering college founded by Gottfried Tulla, the engineer famous for his regulation of the flow of water from the upper Rhine. Tulla had himself studied at the *École Polytechnique* set up in Paris in 1794 to provide technical instruction firmly based on sound scientific training, particularly in mathematics and physics. The *École Polytechnique* can claim to be the original model of the European technological university, and it was Tulla's aim to establish a German counterpart to it. The interesting point is that as well as being an engineer he was also a mathematician and had been appointed to the chair of mathematics at Heidelberg. When the idea of the Karlsruhe polytechnic was mooted the intention was to incorporate it into the university of Heidelberg which was the State university of Baden. Tulla thus had the prospect of a foot in both camps, or to be anachronistic, both campuses. But he resisted this offer, insisting that the two institutions should remain separate, and suggested that he should give up his chair at Heidelberg and become director of the new polytechnic at Karlsruhe. Though in the event he was not appointed to this position he collaborated, as did Weinbrenner, in the setting up of the institution. In this division between the traditional university and the technological sectors of higher education it is interesting to note the reasons given by Tulla for supporting the kind of binary structure that was actually adopted: firstly, that it was more profitable to the State in economic terms; secondly, that two quite separate identities were involved, even mathematics requiring to be taught differently in the two places; thirdly, that the influence of the traditional academics would be detrimental to the development of the specific identity of the new institution.[1] Though these issues arose in the nineteenth century they still stimulate thought in the context of the modern debate about how higher education should be ordered.

Karlsruhe today is a flourishing university with a wide range of activities. The twelve faculties of mathematics, physics, chemistry, bio-

[1] I. Guenther, *A study of the evolution of the German Technische Hochschule,* unpublished. PhD thesis, London University Institute of Education, 1972.

logical and geological sciences, arts and social sciences, architecture, civil engineering, mechanical engineering, chemical engineering, electrical engineering, cybernetics, and economics all incorporate smaller institutes. Within the faculty of physics, for example, are institutes of physics, applied physics, experimental nuclear physics, theoretical physics, theoretical nuclear physics, study of properties of matter, mathematical physics, meteorology, geophysics, and crystallography. In addition there is an inter-faculty Institute of Regional Studies and special units conducting research in the field of high-voltage transmission. Finally, the university works in collaboration with the Karlsruhe nuclear research centre, the federal research centre for nutritional studies, the chemical materials testing office, the Mosbach physics laboratory, and the Centre for Mathematical Education.

The existence of an arts and social sciences faculty will have been noted, and in this context the case of Berlin is instructive. The technological university there resumed its activities after the war at the time of the Nuremberg trials, of which one of the high points was the final address to the court by Albert Speer who had been in charge of armaments and munitions in the Nazi administration from about 1942 and had, incidentally, begun his student career at Karlsruhe. The Germans had been the first to exploit systematically the propaganda potential of wireless, and Speer's observations were concerned with the dangers that technology presented in the hands of the wrong men.

"The nightmare shared by many people that some day the nations of the world may be dominated by technology — that nightmare was very nearly made a reality under Hitler's authoritarian system. Every country in the world today faces the danger of being terrorised by technology, but in a modern dictatorship this seems to me to be unavoidable. Therefore the more technological the world becomes the more essential will be the demand for individual freedom and the self-awareness of the individual human being as a counterpoise to technology."[2]

In thus pointing out the danger of isolating the study of technology from the exploration of social and ethical problems, Speer made a powerful impression on the students of the technological university of

[2] A. Speer, *Inside the Third Reich*, London, 1970, p. 521.

Berlin who against some internal opposition on the part of the professorial staff fought a successful campaign for the establishment of the humanities faculty.

The observation about Karlsruhe and Berlin in the post-war period is broadly speaking true of the other institutions that rank alongside these two – the technological universities of Braunschweig, Hanover, Clausthal, Aachen, Darmstadt, Hohenheim, and Munich. There are nuances of difference in the way they interpret the relationship between humanities, on the one hand, and natural sciences and technology, on the other, largely to do with the degree to which the former are considered subordinate to the latter. And it may be that these nuances are reflected in the designations. Thus, for example, Karlsruhe and Hohenheim use the name *Universität*; Braunschweig, Clausthal, and Hanover call themselves *Technische Universität*; and Munich, Darmstadt, and Aachen have retained the name of *Technische Hochschule*. But these slight variations do not prevent them from forming a coherent and recognisable group.

NEW UNIVERSITIES

With the growth of demand for higher education in the post-war period the existing traditional and technological universities were soon not able to cope with the surge of young people leaving school with the *Abitur* and therefore legally entitled to continue in full-time study. The problem was not solely a numerical one. Particularly in the case of the traditional universities it was a matter of adapting institutions steeped in established values to meet a demand that was much more varied. Among the student population the formerly fairly universal acceptance of the Humboldt ideals of scholarship could no longer be taken for granted. So the new universities founded in the post-war period not only helped to meet sheer numerical demand for places but also were expected to provide opportunities to develop new and flexible programmes that might be more appropriate to the needs of a more heterogeneous clientele.

The need to increase capacity, however, overshadowed the opportunity to promote innovation. For instance, the main reasons given by the parliament of North Rhine-Westphalia for the foundation of the Ruhr university of Bochum were that, firstly, its location about halfway between Cologne and Münster where two of the three existing *Land* universities were sited would facilitate its function to relieve these two overcrowded institutions; secondly, located in the densely populated Ruhr district, it might attract the "ability reserve" in that area, particularly from those social groups for whom the possibility of commuting between home and university might be a decisive factor; thirdly, it would provide a heavily industrialised area with a much-needed cultural centre; and, fourthly, it would establish a better balance between the region of Westphalia which had only the university of Münster and the North Rhine region with Cologne, Bonn, and Aachen.[3]

Innovation was easier in smaller foundations like Bielefeld and Konstanz which set out to pioneer new departmental structures designed to move away from the autocratic ethos of the traditional institutes, to develop the pastoral responsibilities of university teachers, to promote interdisciplinary studies, and to create a favourable environment for research. Konstanz, for example, comprised only three faculties – those of natural sciences, social sciences, and philosophy, with a limit of one thousand students for each. For the social sciences faculty there was to be an establishment of five professors of psychology, five of sociology, five of political science, four of education, six of economics, five of law, and four of statistics. This was a concentration not previously seen in Germany, and remarkable by any standards.[4] Bielefeld was also generously staffed and planned to stimulate research by allowing professors to devote alternate terms to teaching and research. Such favourable conditions were, however, not possible at universities like Bochum which had a much higher number of students and correspondingly large-scale teaching commitments.

OTHER *HOCHSCHULEN*

The compass of higher education in Germany stretches beyond the universities, and a note on terminology is a necessary preliminary to the charting of the remainder of what has become an extensive domain. A common factor is the general designation *Hochschule,* denoting simply an institution of higher education. It will be recalled that the technological

---

[3] E. Böning and K. Roeloffs, *Innovation in Higher Education,* Three German Universities, Paris, OECD, 1970, p. 42.

[4] W. Brezinka, The University of Konstanz, in *Proceedings of the Comparative Education Society in Europe,* Ghent, 1967, p. 193.

universities were traditionally known as *Technische Hochschulen* and that some of them have chosen to retain this name rather than style themselves *Universität.*

In bureaucratic language the term *Wissenschaftliche Hochschule* is used to denote an institution which has the right to grant academic degrees; this category would include, as well as the traditional, technological and new universities, most of the *Pädagogische Hochschulen* or *Erziehungswissenschaftliche Hochschulen* as they are sometimes called, which are the institutions for the education and training of teachers. A further category was created when, as a result of a decision of the *Kultusministerkonferenz,* a number of the leading technical schools (*Fachshulen*) were promoted to the status of *Fachhochschule.* Finally, the institutions of adult education bear the name *Volkshochschule.*

The *Pädagogische Hochschulen* have in most *Länder* had the sole responsibility for the training of elementary teachers. In the early post-war period they were for the most part small autonomous institutions, and as such their viability was called into question. The subsequent trend towards larger units has manifested itself in various ways. One pattern, favoured in North Rhine-Westphalia, has been the grouping of a number of colleges under one parent administration: thus, for example, the *Pädagogische Hochschule Westfalen-Lippe* comprises formerly autonomous institutions sited in Münster and Bielefeld.

Another course has been to follow the long-established Hamburg practice of conducting all teacher training in the university. This has been the case in the university of Giessen in Hesse, for example. And in a few instances the *Pädagogische Hochschule* has been the nucleus around which a new university has been created. Oldenburg and Osnabrück in Lower Saxony are examples. The most far-reaching prospect in this connection, however, is the integration of the *Pädagogische Hochschulen* into the proposed comprehensive higher education structures, the *Gesamthochschulen.*

This is also the prospect before the *Fachhochschulen* which themselves in many cases came into being through the merging of a number of different institutions. While traditionally their province was mainly engineering, the leading ones being known as *Ingenieurschulen,* the new "umbrella" of *Fachhochschule* provides for advanced study in a wider range of fields. This includes: architecture, building, mining/metalworking, chemistry/technical chemistry, electrotechnology, motor engineering, fine mechanical engineering, forestry technology, wood technology, ceramics/ glass technology, nuclear technology, plastics technology, agricultural engineering, food and drinks technology, aircraft engineering, mechanical engineering, milk and dairy technology, physics, production engineering, shipbuilding, ship machinery, health technology, textile technology, and production techniques.[5] Art schools, too, have been incorporated in the new federations. The schools themselves have not always welcomed the resulting loss of identity and, in turn, by no means all of the *Fachhochschulen* are anxious to be incorporated into the larger unit, the *Gesamthochschule.*

The federal law which makes provision for the introduction of these comprehensive structures, the *Hochschulrahmengesetz,* has been fiercely contested, as evidenced by the enormous number of amendments made to the original draft. The case in its favour rests in part on the need to rationalise a sector of which the rapid expansion has been viewed by the general public with no little bewilderment, in part on considerations of egalitarian ideology. Behind the plain desire to do away with the many anomalies born of expansion lie profound controversies over the nature and purpose of higher education. The challenge to the Humboldt model has followed lines that have been familiar in many industrial countries in recent years. Where the traditional approach assumed a higher degree of selectivity the new demand for comprehensiveness meant acceptance of a much wider range of intellectual ability and interest, exploration of new aims, and objectives and of new methods of teaching whereby they could be attained. The *Hochschulrahmengesetz* is therefore a step on the road to mass higher education. It has been designed as a framework within which old academic distinctions – as, for example, between university and specialised higher vocational education – which were strongly identified with social distinctions would become blurred and eventually dissolve. In a word the leitmotiv of the proposed new law was democratisation.

The breaking down of institutional barriers, as well as being seen as a way of getting rid of current notions of status, was intended to facilitate the reorganisation of the content of university level study. Courses were to be less narrowly specialised and this, it was agreed, could more easily be achieved by combining the resources of heterogeneous institutions.

[5] See F. W. Marshall, German intermediate level technical education. *The Vocational Aspect of Education* (Summer, 1973), Vol. XXV, No. 61, pp. 81–82.

Students would not therefore find themselves oriented towards a single profession throughout their university career but would graduate with a polyvalent qualification. Only by following such a strategy, it seemed, could a rational distribution of qualified young people in the labour market be achieved. Also in the interests of rationality was the proposal to set time limits on the permitted periods of study. It has already been noted that traditional academic freedom, as it affected the student population, led to the various abuses associated with the idea of the "eternal student". But reactions to the *Hochschulrahmengesetz* have shown that their freedom is every whit as much prized by students as is the freedom of teaching and research by university staff. The main hope for an untroublesome implementation of the restrictions on time spent at the university — the *Regelstudienzeiten* — would appear to lie, firstly, in a reorganisation of the courses, with their factual content pruned and their objectives realistically designed and spelt out in detail so that students are from the outset aware of what is expected of them; secondly, in increased recognition of the need to expand the pastoral responsibilities of university teachers, for there is little doubt that in the past many students have floundered in their early terms at university for want of help and advice. Another aspect of democratisation has to do with the status and power of individual members of the institutions of higher education. Since the dominant role of the German university professor had reached legendary proportions the new law sought to reduce his powers of patronage and to make more generous provision for a permanent teaching body below professorial rank. This broadening of the basis on which policy decisions are taken was accompanied by a desire to vest greater control of their own affairs in the institutions concerned. The *Gesamthochschulen* were not only to draw up their own research and teaching programmes but were to calculate their own budgets and submit their own development plans.

In summary it can be said that there have been three major variations on the theme of democratisation, namely multidisciplinarity, participation, and autonomy, which equally have been keywords in the reorganisation of higher education in other industrial countries, particularly France. Whether reorganisation will also mean reform depends on how these aims are realised. The danger is obviously that the creation of *Gesamthochschulen* will in practice turn out to be predominantly an administrative merger with few results in terms of genuine academic co-operation between formerly separate institutions.

Whatever the fate of the *Hochschulrahmengesetz* in the *Bundestag* — and the prospects for its enactment must be considered slender — it seems clear that the way in which integration takes place will depend on the specific legislation of the individual *Länder*. And since in some of them the process is already under way there will soon be evidence on which to assess the success of the venture. In North Rhine-Westphalia, for example, the first five *Gesamthochschulen* were opened in 1972 by merging existing *Pädagogische Hochschulen* with *Fachhochschulen*. The official intention is to add the universities into the new structures by 1977.

CHAPTER 8

The Teaching Profession

The *Strukturplan* of 1970 which conceived of the school system of the Federal Republic as being built up in successive stages — elementary, primary, lower secondary, and upper secondary — was all things to all men. While it bore the imprint of horizontally structured comprehensiveness it was designed in such a way that its recommendations regarding an examinations and qualifications structure could be just as easily put into effect in the context of the traditional tripartite system as through the introduction of *Gesamtschulen.* Thus this plan and the *Bildungsgesamtplan* which followed in 1973 both glossed over the fundamental differences that existed between *Länder* with regard to the future of the school system. Both were able to claim a commonality of purpose in educational reform even though there were diametrically opposed views as to the means of achieving it. But these opposed views did not yet engender any serious divisiveness by comparison with other Western European countries, for the advent of *Gesamtschulen* was very slow. The pattern in the overwhelmingly larger part of the Federal Republic remained one that comprised different types of school, and it was easy enough to superimpose the overall conception of stages upon it.

What proved to be much more contentious was the issue of the training of the teachers who were to serve in a "staged" system. When the controversy over the reorganisation of the training and the qualifications and remuneration structure of the teaching profession reached its peak it was the most divisive issue that had arisen throughout the post-war period and one which at one point threatened to bring to an end the years of co-operation between the *Länder* in matters of educational policy.

THE DIVISION IN THE TEACHING PROFESSION

At the root of the problem lies the long-standing distinction between the *Gymnasium* teacher, who has completed a university education and professional training analagous to that required for the legal profession, and the elementary school teacher, the *Volksschullehrer*, who has, generally speaking, not had a highly academic education at university but has been professionally trained at a *Pädagogische Hochschule*. The distinction is given semantic reinforcement by the fact that the *Gymnasium* teacher is known as *Studienrat* and has the further prospect of rising to *Oberstudienrat, Fachdirektor, Gymnasialprofessor*, and, as head of a school, *Oberstudiendirektor*, a hierarchy of titles which is beyond the reach of those in the lower echelons of the profession. The best career prospect for most primary school teachers has lain in the opportunity to acquire sufficient further qualifications to be appointed to teach in a *Realschule*. Those who had done so tended to hold just as tenaciously to their status as did the *Gymnasium* teachers so that attitudes in these divisions of the profession tended to confirm the divisions in the school system. There has, it is true, been some blurring at the edges of the distinction between university and non-university educated teachers, as, for example, in Hamburg, where all teacher training has for many years been carried on within the university, and more generally in the growth of the provision whereby university students could graduate as *Realschule* rather than *Gymnasium* teachers. None the less, the fundamental controversy over the relationship of education as a subject of study to university-level work as a whole has dominated post-war discussion of the organisation of the education and training of teachers up to the present day.

Many interested parties have agreed that an academic education for all teachers is essential in order to keep pace with educational and more general social change. But the universities while endorsing this view in principle have appeared reluctant to accept the inference that the *Pädagogische Hochschulen* should therefore be integrated into their particular sector. This reluctance recalls the kind of division over the issue that has been evident among university teachers in other western European countries. Some factions within the university sector go so far as to reject the notion that an academic training is at all necessary or desirable for teachers in *Grundschulen* or *Hauptschulen,* claiming that student teachers for these levels are less able than university students and that the majority of them have no interest in academic disciplines. The acceptance of education as a field of study within universities is seen in these quarters as the thin end of the wedge towards a situation where university work could become dominated by the requirements of teacher training, to the detriment of scholarship.

Nearer the centre of the debate, however, is the question of the relative weight to be given to the subjects that future teachers will be concerned with in the schools and to the study of education *per se.* The universities tend, naturally enough, to be preoccupied with the importance of the former, the *Pädagogische Hochschulen* with the latter, and this relates very closely to the distinction between *Studienrat* and *Volksschullehrer.* Symbolised in down-to-earth fashion by differing salary scales and conditions of service, the distinction rested not only on the greater prestige of established academic disciplines as compared with educational studies but also on the length of time required to qualify for the respective branches of the teaching profession. The average period required to reach the *Staatsexamen* in a university has been six years, followed then by a two year *Referendariat* made up of probationary teaching together with the study of educational theory and method. Thus the newly qualified *Studienrat* is likely to be not far off 30 years of age. The *Volksschullehrer,* on the other hand, has only three-year full-time training before becoming a probationary teacher, and so can expect to begin a career considerably earlier than his or her counterpart in the *Gymnasium.* In order for a structure of the teaching profession to correspond to the conditions set out in the *Strukturplan* these two conceptions would need to be reconciled, and since university studies are generally held to be too long drawn out in Germany it is clearly in the syllabuses of the academic disciplines that the reductions are most likely to be sought.

THE *STUFENLEHRER* CONTROVERSY

In 1970 a degree of consensus appeared to have been arrived at by the *Kultusministerkonferenz* in the Frankenthal Agreement which attempted to set out the conditions for a unitary system for the training of teachers. Some of the elements in this were straightforward re-statements of existing practice or of earlier points of agreement regarding changes; others were to prove highly controversial. According to the declaration, preparation for teaching at all levels of the school system should be conducted at institutions of university level – the term used for this was *wissenschaftliche Hochschulen* – and in two phases, both terminated by a State examination.

The first phase was to comprise, as before, full-time study; the second was to be a *Referendariat* of the kind hitherto demanded of *Gymnasium* teachers and now extended to embrace the entire school-teaching profession. The two phases were to be closely related to one another. The content was to be made up of educational studies and of main and subsidiary specialisms though it was not made clear to which of the two sectors the methodology of specialist subject teaching belonged.

The controversial part of the declaration lay in the proposal to replace previous categories by three new grades of teacher, for primary, lower secondary, and upper secondary levels, with a further distinction between a basic first phase of three years' and an extended first phase of four years' duration. The content of the courses was to vary with the respective levels. For teaching at the primary stage, the *Primarstufe*, the requirement was the basic educational studies course, a further more penetrating course in educational studies and a main subject course; the time allocation was to be in the ratio 1:1:1. For the extended four-year course for the *Primarstufe* a second specialist teaching subject was to be added, equivalent in weighting to the first three. For the lower secondary stage, *Sekundarstufe I*, in addition to the basic educational studies two subject specialisms were required, the three components again to be in the ratio 1:1:1, while the extended four-year course required a doubling of the weighting of one of the subject specialisms so that one became "main", the other "subsidiary". Thus the extension from a three-year to a four-year period of study could only be made by the way of additional study of academic subjects to be subsequently taught in schools. Finally, for the upper secondary stage, *Sekundarstufe II,* the basic educational studies course together with a main subject in the ratio 1:2 was proposed. Some *Länder*, however, wished to insist that preparation for teaching at this level should be exclusively on a four-year basis and comprise education and main and subsidiary subjects in the ratio 1:2:1.

Thus with the Frankenthal statement the idea of the *Stufenlehrer* was launched on the basis of a fairly general agreement, but in the details of how the scheme was to be implemented a deep division of attitudes was evident. The aim of the keenest advocates of the idea, notably the *Gewerkschaft Erziehung und Wissenschaft*, the trade union which mainly represented the interests of primary teachers, was to establish uniform conditions of service and remuneration for teachers at all three levels in the school system; according to this view, a higher salary grade would depend not on the type of school in which the post was held but on the length of the period of training and would therefore be equally accessible to all three grades. Though it is a very old idea that the best-paid teachers should be those who teach the youngest age groups, suggestions that it should be put into practice have generally been disregarded. The principle that remuneration in teaching should be hierarchically graded on the basis of qualifications and the academic level at which instruction is given has seldom been seriously challenged. The proposal that the same grading scheme should be applied to teachers at all three levels in the school system was too much for some of the *Länder* to accept; in their view the academic requirements for teaching at the upper secondary level justified a higher level of salary, and this should be accessible to primary and lower secondary teachers only if they acquired the relevant academic qualifications.

Looked at from another angle the controversy was over the question of whether or not teachers with only a three-year training and one subject specialism to offer were acceptable within the upper secondary stage. The division of opinion over the issue followed clearly defined political party lines. Those *Länder* which had *CDU/CSU* governments were determined to retain a requirement for higher academic qualifications for the upper secondary level, based on four years of full-time study and a subsidiary as well as a main subject. The *SPD*-controlled *Länder* on the other hand — West Berlin, Hamburg, Bremen, Hesse, North Rhine-Westphalia, and Lower Saxony — wished to introduce the *Stufenlehrer* principle in its fully egalitarian form. At a meeting in Hamburg in 1972 their education ministers concluded an agreement to go ahead with this policy. The agreement also provided for mutual acceptance of the *Stufenlehrer* pattern of qualifications, and herein lay the most serious implication for educational policy within the Federal Republic as a whole. For the *CDU/CSU Länder* were not prepared to accept the new qualifications pattern *in toto*, and the prospect was therefore opened up that there would no longer be complete mobility of the teaching profession throughout the country but that, according to the view taken of their qualifications, teachers would be restricted to employment within one or other of the two groups. It was just such restrictions on inter-*Land* mobility that much of post-war educational policy had been designed to remove or avoid.

In fact, however, extreme confrontation over the issues involved appears likely to be averted because of financial considerations. While there is perhaps a possibility of improving the conditions of service for lower secondary teachers, the cost of upgrading primary teachers to a state of parity with their secondary colleagues would be so vast – estimated at between DM500 and 600 million in the case of North Rhine-Westphalia[1] – as to make the proposal quite unrealistic. This in turn makes it more likely that the provision whereby upper secondary teachers are required to have spent four years in full-time study will be fairly generally accepted, as is, for example, the case in the proposals for the introduction of *Stufenlehrer* training as from 1975 in North Rhine-Westphalia. These proposals follow the Frankenthal guidelines. Future *Sekundarstufe II* teachers are to devote one-quarter of their time to educational studies, a further quarter to their subsidiary, and half to their main subject. For *Sekundarstufe I* the time is to be divided into a third each for educational studies, main, and subsidiary subjects, and a tripartite division is also proposed for the *Primarstufe*. The probationary period under the plan is to last one year for primary teachers and eighteen months for the two secondary stages, with a provision to reduce the latter period to eight months for the duration of the current teacher shortage.[2]

THE SUPPLY OF TEACHERS

The shortage of teachers is a factor that has cast a large shadow over education policy in recent years. It was difficult for existing programmes of teacher training to keep pace with the expansion of the school population in the late 1960s. Now this wave has reached the threshold of higher education at a time of lean employment prospects for graduates, and the

[1] *Bildung und Wissenschaft*, 13-73, p. 8.
[2] *Ibid*., pp. 7–8.

numbers of school-leavers wishing to become teachers has steadily risen to a point where a surplus of teachers is in prospect. One of the early predictions of this, made by the Conference of Finance Ministers of the *Länder*, tended to be interpreted as a ploy on their part to discourage expansion in higher education and thereby reduce pressure on their *Land* budgets. Their theme can, however, be buttressed by statistics. School enrolments show a downward trend in all but the three *Länder* of West Berlin, Hamburg, and Hesse, and in these the increase has been slight. When this situation is set against the increases in student numbers – from 7·4 per cent of the age cohort in 1960 to 21·1 per cent in 1974 – and the rising demand for places in *Pädagogische Hochschulen*, a surplus of teachers becomes more than speculation.[3] An extensive survey carried out by the *Kultusministerium* of North Rhine-Westphalia has indicated that, even allowing for the improvements in teacher–pupil ratios assumed in the *Bildungsgesamtplan,* for example a reduction from 33 to 22 in the case of the primary sector, present trends will bring about an excess of teachers for all types of school except *Realschulen* and *Berufsschulen.*[4]

It will obviously be beneficial if the excess of manpower can be diverted into these two sectors which have suffered from the most chronic staff shortages in the recent past, particularly so if at the same time teacher–pupil ratios become more favourable, though it should be pointed out that the advantages will largely be neutralised if there is not a corresponding increase in the number of classrooms provided. Many schools are more short of space than of teachers.

THE EDUCATION AND TRAINING OF TEACHERS

The question arises to what extent the new trend will affect the nature of the education and training given to teachers. The problems experienced in this respect in Germany differ little from those to be observed in other countries. The ideal can be stated platitudinously: that every teacher should have an academic education that can genuinely be considered as of university standard, and also a professional training that is adequate to guarantee competence in the classroom. To return to the discussion begun earlier, the inevitable disputes arise over what constitutes an academic

[3] *Neue Hannoversche Zeitung,* 20.9.74.
[4] *Die Welt,* 6.11.74.

education; whether, for example, educational studies pursued at degree level are acceptable as the academic cachet, or whether it is right to insist that the emphasis should be on the subjects that can subsequently be taught in schools. Where a stipulation of the latter kind may have been unrealistic when a rise in the recruitment of teachers was an urgent requirement, it becomes more conceivable in a competitive situation where the number of places is limited. Furthermore, it could be implemented with discrimination as a result of the greater flexibility that is being introduced into the upper secondary curriculum and which was analysed in Chapter 5. This curricular change greatly reduces the danger of losing promising teachers because of encylopedic entrance demands. Thus with the move away from the requirement that the *Abiturient* should be a polymath, the new possibilities for specialisation at upper secondary level bring the prospect that entrants to the *Pädagogische Hochschulen* will show a higher standard of achievement in the disciplines they are later to teach in schools. There can be little doubt that this would be a healthy development as regards the quality of teaching and, furthermore, that it would advance the academic ambitions of the *Pädagogische Hochschulen.*

These ambitions, however, have the effect of pushing the emphasis away from school subjects in the direction of educational studies. Westfalen-Lippe which, along with the other two large *Pädagogische Hochschulen* in North Rhine-Westphalia, those of the Ruhr and the Rhineland, represents a fairly advanced stage in the realisation of the academic aspirations of the teacher-training sector provides a convenient illustration. Here one-half of the student's time is devoted to the *Grundstudium*, or foundation study, which

"deals with education under the two aspects of general pedagogy and school pedagogy, as well as psychology, philosophy, sociology, political science according to choice. It provides the foundations for a critical understanding of the problems of education in the present-day world and the present-day school; it contributes to the integration of specialist subject and 'staged level' studies in the total context of the education course."[5]

[5] Pädagogische Hochschule Westfalen-Lippe, *Personal- und Vorlesungsverzeichnis,* Sommersemeter, 1974, p. 18.

The student devotes a further third of his or her time to the specialist subject and at the end of the course is qualified to teach it at all levels of the *Grundschule* and the *Hauptschule*. Finally, the remaining sixth of the time is claimed by the studies especially related to the stage in the system at which the student wishes to teach, such as primary or lower secondary, for example. It is clear from this programme that the *Pädagogische Hochschulen* take a different view from that of the universities in the question of where the emphasis should be placed if the academic quality of teacher training is to be improved. The new law in North Rhine-Westphalia referred to earlier will not alter the existing balance much, and since it follows the Frankenthal guidelines it can be considered fairly representative of current thinking in the Federal Republic as a whole.

Yet the reluctance to emphasise single-subject specialisms needs to be examined further. Central to the justification of it is the growth of inter-disciplinary curricula, and this development is sometimes seen as the symbol of a wider cultural change, some kind of relationship being assumed to exist between the established hierarchy of disciplines and the social class structure. The lines of demarcation are not only seen as indi-vidual frontiers between the disciplines themselves but also collectively as a barrier which makes them inaccessible to the majority of the school population. To break down these barriers through interdisciplinary work is, it is argued, to promote the cause of democracy by ceasing to design education with the benefits for a mainly middle-class minority in mind, but rather by adapting it to the needs of a working-class majority which does not share the traditional assumptions about academic values. For the teacher who is setting about this task the prevalent view is that the emphasis in training should be on educational studies, while a less intensive study of the traditional school subjects is sufficient as a basis for teaching in an interdisciplinary fashion.

This kind of proposition tends to appear self-evident in teacher training circles, especially as it is obvious enough that there are alternative ways of organising knowledge and that there is a political element involved in the desire to retain the traditional subject structure. But the cultural change that it seeks to promote may be less enthusiastically endorsed in society at large. This discrepancy is healthy in that it promotes a creative relationship between schools and society. Yet if the gap is too great, if the aims of teachers are too unrealistic in terms of the down to earth requirements of the outside world with respect to the basic skills that children learn, then there is a danger that the professional education and training given in the *Pädagogische Hochschulen* will simply be discredited. As with politicians, it is the task of teachers to lead rather than to follow public opinion; but when they lead by too great a distance their influence is correspondingly reduced. The excessive pursuit of social scientific insights at the expense of work on the subjects to be taught in school is a danger both in Germany and elsewhere. What is important is the relationship between the two. The need to get it right is fundamental.

It is from this perspective that the future structure of the education and training of teachers must be viewed. The relationship between the *Pädagogische Hochschulen* and the universities is at issue in the debate over the future of higher education, as was seen in the last chapter. As to the prospects in the context of the *Gesamthochschule* there should be no underestimation of the obstacles to a worthwhile integration, one in which both sides would agree on a joint approach to the problem of a curriculum for the training of teachers. The danger is that such changes as do take place will be more in name than in substance. But if the situation is uncertain and probably unpromising, it is not final. A significant development which leads out of the impasse is the growth of in-service training for teachers at a later stage in their careers. The most encouraging feature of the vast programme launched in 1974 along lines pioneered by the Open University in England is that it is in response to demands from the teachers themselves. This kind of continuing education and training seems more likely to foster the growth of an effective teaching force than the negotiations over the future structure of higher education.

CHAPTER 9

Review and Outlook

The foregoing chapters have shown how difficult it is to make general observations about the Federal Republic of Germany, in particular with respect to education. Reservations have constantly to be made to the effect that it is the responsibility of individual *Länder*, that it reflects such differences as between north and south, urban agglomeration and rural expanse, the religious and the secular, the conservative and the social democratic, the older generation and the younger. And yet for all the reservations one is left with certain abiding impressions and it is possible to indulge in speculation about the course that educational development will take in the coming years.

Overriding all other generalisations about West Germany is its deep-seated conservatism, the thread of which can be followed throughout the history of its education. Indeed, there is a temptation to think that it has been an unshakable respect for past achievements and traditional virtues on the part of the great majority of the population that has spurred the proponents of radicalism to such extremes of commitment. The radical tradition in education has been upheld by champion after champion from Froebel to Oestreich, and its byproducts have been some of the most perceptive and convincing pieces of writing to be found in the literature of education. Yet it never succeeded in making anything but a mild impression on the way the country has gone about educating its children. It would be a daunting essay in cultural and political history to attempt to explain this. What can be suggested with some confidence is that at the time when the teaching profession fulfilled a leading role in society its members, whatever the kind of school they were in, were, on the whole, steeped in conservative attitudes and authoritarian methods; and that in more recent times when there has been a greater tendency in some sectors of the profession to adopt a more radical political stance, teachers have, on the whole, carried less weight in society than in the past.

The conservatism in respect of education is, of course, a part of the wider spectrum of national politics. The twenty years or so of *CDU/CSU* dominance in the *Bundestag* after the creation of the Federal Republic consolidated traditional attitudes and structures, reinforcing the long-standing aversion to experimentation. Flashiness, whether in domestic architecture, saloon cars, or reform programmes, was alien to the German spirit; thoroughness and proven reliability were the qualities that were prized above all. And certainly in the post-war years these solid virtues appeared to bring their just reward. The Federal Republic thrived. With West Berlin as its brightly lit shop window it outshone its drab estranged sibling, the *DDR*. Not surprisingly, the general satisfaction that accompanied such clearly observable success included satisfaction with the education system.

Yet all was not as well as it seemed. The impressively well-qualified and industrious labour force owed no small degree of its vitality and drive to the injection of able and highly motivated manpower arriving via the West Berlin refugee route from the *DDR*. It seems likely that it was by and large the more enterprising and clever citizens, many of them middle-class victims of discriminatory legislation, who migrated westwards. The Federal Republic absorbed them easily and without any great conscious realisation of how much their contribution disguised weaknesses in an education system which attracted little serious criticism.

Abruptly this source of supply ceased with the erection of the Berlin Wall in 1961. Henceforth the Federal Republic was on its own, and as the years went by shortages of labour at the more highly qualified levels began to be felt. Now this cannot, of course, solely be attributed to the drying up of the eastern source. As pointed out in Chapter 3, the gap left by the war was beginning to be felt as retirement age overtook an earlier generation which had not suffered such heavy losses in combat and had consequently been able to play a disproportionate part in manning the various sectors of the nation's economic life. Also, the expansion of technology and the changes in the structure of society explored in the same chapter increased the quantitative requirements in the more educated echelons. At any rate, whatever the precise combination of factors, the situation was rapidly transformed from one of contentment to one of concern, if not indeed dismay.

This concern was the signal for dissatisfaction which had rumbled well below the surface to erupt into strident demands for change supported by plausible statistics presaging collapse and passionate denunciation, of a social hierarchy dedicated, it was claimed, to the educational oppression of the working class. The turmoil in education can be seen in retrospect as part of a more general resurgence of socialism in politics. True, the *SPD* had always had its strongholds, controlling or strongly influencing more often than not the government in the city states and in *Länder* such as Hesse and Lower Saxony. But the fact of *CDU/CSU* dominance in the *Bundestag* had in practice restricted their ability to diverge greatly from the general conservative consensus.

The later 1960s, however, saw the gradual rise to power of the *SPD*, first in the notorious "Grand Coalition" which provoked such an outcry among the student population, then in coalition with the *FDP*. The *SPD* rose on a tide of reform demands which gathered momentum at what was for Germany a bewildering speed. In education the new government began to flex its federal muscles with a view to substituting socialist planning on a national scale for the pragmatic *laissez-faire* approach of its predecessors. Where the activities of supra-*Land* bodies like the *Bildungsrat* had followed a relatively unobtrusive path which seemed as likely as not to lead to the waste ground of political apathy, they now began to bask in the glare of favourable publicity. With the publication of such documents as the *Strukturplan,* the *Bildungsbericht,* and the *Bildungsgesamtplan* within the space of a few years a veritable planomania had set in. Politically speaking, this phase was accompanied by a drive, never previously evident in Germany, to bring in the kind of structural changes that had become commonplace elsewhere in Europe. Most of the plans carried an indication that they lent themselves to implementation particularly within the framework of the *Gesamtschule.* The general vogue for reorganisation along comprehensive lines extended to teacher training in the form of the *Stufenlehrer* plan and to the entire domain of higher education for which a new comprehensive law was drafted, the *Hochschulrahmengesetz.*

Despite its growing intervention in educational policy, however, the federal government has still had to reckon with the obduracy of those *Länder* with conservative governments which are not prepared to accept the comprehensive theses. The authors of the various plans have moved heaven and earth to create an impression of agreement and unity of purpose by the use of such blanket terms as *Sekundarstufe* and *Sekundarbereich,* but this only disguises the serious divisions over principle that still exist. In the days of the *SPD*'s demoralisation which culminated in its *Godesberger Programm* — the electoral programme which set the seal on the party's abandonment of Marxist ideas — it had, even when in strength at *Land* level, been poorly positioned to challenge the prevailing conservative consensus. Now, though the positions have been reversed, the balance of power is more delicate, and the *CDU/CSU* have been able defiantly to resist the radical reform programmes. The consequence of this has been the appearance of the greatest schism ever in the politics of education in the Federal Republic. The *Bildungsgesamtplan,* it will be recalled, was obliged to distinguish at various points between the views of the federation and six *Länder,* on the one hand, and the remaining five *Länder,* on the other. Thus the effect of the great reform surge of the 1960s has not by any means been to shatter post-war restoration policy throughout the country. Even the breaches which it has made in the wall of conservatism can by no means be regarded as permanent.

On the whole, time has worked against the radicals. Much of what has been said about social change based on educational opportunity has been belied by the facts, as observed impressionistically by the great majority of the population. The longer the case for change is presented to the public, while the situation in fact remains that the *Gymnasium* is the *Gymnasium* is the *Gymnasium* . . ., whether it is called that or not, the more the general public tends to regard educational crusades as displays of rhetoric. This waiting game is currently what characterises the politics of education in the Federal Republic. With every year that passes the objurgations of soothsayers such as Georg Picht attract more ridicule and the idealistic lustre of the Brandt era becomes tarnished. The greater the euphoria, the greater the potential disillusionment, and the risk that this holds for the entire reform enterprise is obvious. Even within the *SPD* itself the accession of Helmut Schmidt has shown the straws that are in the wind. Sober realistic assessments of priorities are obviously what are required in order to hold the electoral line in readiness for the 1976 contest. In this situation of stalemate the *CDU/CSU* waits in the wings gathering its support in the hope that the time-honoured conservatism of the country will reassert itself.

How important a role educational policy will play in the political contests of the later 1970s is not easy to predict. Interest in *Bildungspolitik* has certainly waned. In the less-charged climate that has resulted, however, it is no doubt clear to both major protagonists that the chief misjudgment of the recent era has been the relative neglect of the vocational sector in the headlong pursuit of impressive *Abitur* quotas. The contention that the intellectual potential of the nation could be measured by the proportion of *Abiturienten* was a denial of the educational forces that had fashioned German economic success in the past. It was quite clearly not the quantity of *Abiturienten* that was important, and though their quality was no doubt an asset, what was really crucial was the quality of the labour force, from the engineer to the skilled worker. The true debate is about finding a rationale for the revitalisation of vocational education and training. In one view it is most likely to come about in a school system increasingly made up of *Gesamtschulen*, providing a framework within which general and vocational education can be integrated. In the other view, structural reorganisation doing away with the *Gymnasium* is a red herring, diverting attention from the immediate task of providing the manpower required in industry, which, it is claimed, is best achieved through the modification of the traditional patterns of provision. Whichever faction wins the day the problem is essentially the same. It is the means rather than the end that are in dispute.

Glossary

Abendgymnasium: *Gymnasium* for part-time evening study.
Abendrealschule: *Realschule* for part-time evening study.
Abitur: leaving certificate of *Gymnasium*.
Abiturient: pupil in final year of study at *Gymnasium*.
Abschluss: leaving certificate.
allgemein: general.
Allgemeinbildung/allgemeine Bildung: general education in the Humboldt tradition.
altsprachlich: concerned with classical languages.
Arbeitslehre: pre-vocational sector of the school curriculum.
Arbeitsschule: "activity school" as pioneered by Georg Kerschensteiner.
Aufbaugymnasium: "late start" *Gymnasium*.
Ausbau: expansion.
Ausbildung: training.
ausreichend: adequate.
Ausschuss: committee.
Auszeichnung: excellence.

baccalauréat: leaving certificate of French *lycée*.
befriedigend: creditable.
Beobachtungsstufe: observation/orientation stage.
Beratungslehrer: teacher responsible for advising pupils on curricular and vocational choices.
Berufsaufbauschule: type of vocational school.
Berufsbild: trade profile.
Berufsbildungsgesetz: law concerning vocational education.
Berufsfachschule: type of vocational school.
Berufsgrundbildungsjahr: year of pre-vocational education.
Berufsgrundschule: school for the *Berufsgrundbildungsjahr*.
Berufsoberschule: variant of the *Fachoberschule*.
Berufsschule: vocational school for part-time study, usually in conjunction with apprenticeship.
bestanden: passed (examination).
Bildung: education, particularly in the sense of acquisition of knowledge and refinement of aesthetic appreciation. Cf. *Erziehung*.
Bildungsbericht: report on education.
Bildungsgesamtplan: all-embracing plan for education.
Bildungskatastrophe: educational catastrophe.
Bildungsplanung: educational planning.
Bildungspolitik: educational policy.

152   *Glossary*

Bild:ingsrat: Education Council.
Bildungswesen: educational system.
Buchschule: book school, pejorative term used by Georg Kerschensteiner.
Bund: federation.
Bund entschiedener Schulreformer: League of Radical School Reformers.
Bund-Länder-Kommission: Federal-*Land* Commission.
Bundeselternrat: federal council of parents' associations.
Bundesrat: upper house of federal parliament.
Bundestag: lower house of federal parliament.

CDU (Christlich Demokratische Union): Christian Democratic Party (Conservative Party).
CSU (Christlich Soziale Union): Bavarian wing of *CDU*.

DDR (Deutsche Demokratische Republik): Democratic Republic of Germany (East Germany).
Demokratisierung: democratisation.
deutsch: German.
Deutsche Heimschule: German boarding school, a Nazi creation.
Deutsche Oberschule: type of secondary school created in the 1920s, later much favoured by the Nazis.
Deutsche Schule: German school.
Deutscher Ausschuss: German Committee (for Education).
Deutscher Landerziehungsheim: independent boarding school sited in rural surroundings.
Deutscher Lehrerverein: German Teachers' Union.
Deutsches Volk: German people.
Doktorprüfung: examination for the doctorate.
Drittelparität: tripartite division of voting rights in universities.

École Polytechnique: polytechnical school founded in Paris in 1794.
Einheitsschule: general term for comprehensive school or comprehensive school system.
Einrichtung: institution.
Elementarbereich: domain of pre-school education.
Entwicklung: development.
Erlebnis: experience.
Erziehung: education in the general sense of upbringing. Cf. *Bildung.*
Erziehungswissenschaft: the academic study of education.
Erziehungswissenschaftliche Hochschule: college for the education and training of teachers.

Fach: academic subject.
Fachdirektor: head of department.
fachgebunden: restricted to certain subjects.
Fachgymnasium: *Gymnasium* not offering the orthodox range of academic subjects.
Fachhochschule: institution of higher vocational studies.
Fachidiot: "specialist idiot".
Fachoberschule: vocational alternative to upper stage of *Gymnasium.*

Glossary 153

Fachschulreife: qualification for entry to certain categories of vocational school.
FDP (Freie Demokratische Partei): Free Democratic Party (Liberal Party).
F-Gymnasium: see *Fachgymnasium.*
Förderstufe: two-year observation and guidance stage between primary and secondary school.
Förderung: promotion.
Fortbildungsschule: continuation school.
frauenberuflich: concerned with professions practised by women.
Freie Schulgemeinde: Free School Community.

Ganztagsschule: whole-day school.
Gastarbeiter: immigrant worker.
Gemeinde: parish, commune.
Gesamthochschule: comprehensive university.
Gesamtschule: comprehensive school.
Gesetz: law.
Gewerkschaft: trade union.
Godesberger Programm: political programme of *SPD* agreed at 1959 conference in Bad Godesberg.
Grundschule: primary school.
Grundstudium: foundation course of study.
gymnasiale Oberstufe: upper sector of *Gymnasium.*
Gymnasialprofessor: title conferred on distinguished *Gymnasium* teachers.
Gymnasium: grammar school (academic secondary school).

Habilitation: test of recognition as university teacher on a permanent basis.
Hauptschule: new kind of secondary school, a development of the upper classes of the *Volksschule.*
Hauswirtschaft: domestic science.
Hochschule: institution of higher education.
Hochschulrahmengesetz: higher education law.
Hochschulreife: fitness for university study; (a) *allgemeine Hochschulreife* attested by full *Abitur,* traditionally giving right of access to any faculty; (b) *fachgebundene Hochschulreife,* attested by reduced *Abitur,* access being restricted to certain faculties.

Ingenieurschule: school of engineering.

Jahrgang: year cohort.
Jahrgangsklasse: class of pupils kept together for all instruction throughout their school career.

Keine Experimente: No experiments.
Klassenlehrer: form teacher.
Kolleg: institution of further education for acquisition of *Abitur* on a full-time basis.
kooperativ: co-operative.
Kreis: 1 (as in *Ettlinger Kreis*), discussion group; 2, local administrative district.
Kulturkunde: study of (German) culture.
Kultusministerkonferenz: Conference of *Land* Ministers of Education.

Land, *plural* **Länder:** constituent State of Federal Republic.
Landerziehungsheim: see *Deutscher Landerziehungsheim.*
Landwirtschaft: agriculture.
Lehrfreiheit: freedom to teach.
Leistung: achievement.
Lernfreiheit: freedom to learn.

Magisterprüfung: examination for master's degree.
mangelhaft: poor.
mathematisch: mathematical.
Mein Kampf: *My Struggle,* book by Adolf Hitler.
Menschenserziehung: *The Education of Man,* book by Friedrich Froebel.
Mittelbau: collective term for university junior teaching staff.
Mitteldeutschland: Middle Germany.
Mittelpunktschule: central school serving a number of rural communities.
Mittelschule: intermediate school.
Mittelstufe: intermediate stage of a school system.
mittlere Reife: intermediate qualification/leaving certificate.
musisch: concerned with the arts.

Nationalpolitische Erziehungsanstalt: National Socialist Party School.
naturwissenschaftlich: concerned with natural sciences.
Neugestaltung: reshaping.
neusprachlich: concerned with modern languages.
Notenarithmetik: pejorative term for the arithmetic of grading systems.
numerus clausus: restricted number, with reference to candidates admitted for study at university faculties and departments.

Oberrealschule: historical term for non-classical secondary school.
Oberschule: secondary school.
Oberstudiendirektor: headmaster of *Gymnasium.*
Oberstudienrat: senior teacher at a *Gymnasium.*
Oberstufe: upper stage; generally used with reference to upper classes of *Volksschule* or *Gymnasium.*
Orientierungsstufe: orientation stage.

Pädagogische Hochschule: college for the education and training of teachers.
Polytechnische Schule: polytechnical school.
praxisnah: closely concerned with practice.
Primarbereich: domain of primary education.
Probeunterricht: trial teaching.
Produktionsschule: production school.

Rahmenplan: outline plan for the school system put forward by the *Deutscher Ausschuss* in 1959.
Realgymnasium: historical term for non-classical secondary school.
Realschule: intermediate school.
Referendariat: period of initial in-service teacher training.
Regelstudienzeiten: limitations on time spent following university courses, as proposed in *Hochschulrahmengesetz.*

Reich: empire.
Reifeprüfung: school-leaving examination.
Restauration: restoration, term used to denote post-war policy of conservative
    character.

Schule: school.
Schülermitverwaltung: participation of pupils in school governance and admin-
    istration.
Schulpflicht: period of compulsory school attendance.
Sekundarbereich: domain of secondary education.
Sekundarschulwesen: secondary school system.
Sekundarstufe: secondary stage.
sitzen bleiben: to "stay down", i.e. to be denied promotion to the next class at the
    beginning of the new school year.
Sonderschule: special school.
Sozialwissenschaft: social science.
SPD (Sozialdemokratische Partei Deutschlands): Social Democratic Party.
Spiegel: mirror; Der Spiegel: weekly newspaper.
Sprachenfolge: sequence in which foreign languages are taught.
Sprechstunde: period for consultation of teachers by parents.
Staatsexamen: State examination.
Strukturplan: structural plan for the education system put forward by the
    Bildungsrat in 1970.
Studienrat: teacher in a Gymnasium.
Studienschule: proposed designation for academic secondary school with classics-
    biased curriculum (Rahmenplan, 1959).
Studierfähigkeit: fitness to pursue university study.
Stufenausbildung: rationalised system of vocational training.
Stufenlehrer: teacher trained for service in a specific stage of the school system.

technisch: technical, technological.

ungenügend: weak.
Universität: university.

venia legendi: "indulgence to read", authorisation to teach in a university on a
    permanent basis.
Vereinbarung: agreement.
Versuch: trial.
Vielwisserei: indiscriminating accumulation of factual knowledge.
Volk: people.
Volkshochschule: institution for advanced level adult education.
Volksschule: elementary school.
Volksschullehrer: elementary school teacher.
volkstümlich: popular.

Wandervögel: lit. birds of passage; used in the sense of ramblers or hikers to denote
    members of the Youth Movement of the early twentieth century.
wirtschaftswissenschaftlich: concerned with economics.

Wissenschaft: science; field of academic study.
Wissenschaftsrat: Council for Education and Science.

Zeit: time; **Die Zeit:** weekly newspaper.
Zupfgeigenhansl: song book of the Youth Movement.

Bibliography

SELECTED BIBLIOGRAPHY OF WORKS IN ENGLISH

Alexander, L. and Parker, B., *The New Education in the German Republic,* New York, 1929.

Arnold, M., *Higher Schools and Universities in Germany,* London, 1892.

Board of Education, *Special Reports on Educational Subjects,* vol. 3, London, 1898; vol. 9, London, 1902.

Böning, E. and Roeloffs, K., *Innovation in Higher Education: Three German Universities,* Paris, 1970.

Dahrendorf, R., *Society and Democracy in Germany,* London, 1968.

Führ, C. and Halls, W. D. (eds.), *Educational Reform in the Federal Republic of Germany,* Hamburg, 1970.

Hearnden, A., *Education in the Two Germanies,* Oxford, 1974.

Helmreich, E. C., *Religious Education in German Schools,* Harvard, 1959.

Kohn, H., *The Mind of Germany,* London, 1961.

Laqueur, W. Z., *Young Germany,* London, 1962.

Lawson, R. F., *The Reform of the West German School System,* Ann Arbor, 1965.

Lynch, J. and Plunkett, H. D., *Teacher Education and Cultural Change,* London, 1973.

Mann, E., *School for Barbarians,* London, 1939.

OECD Reviews of National Policies for Education, *Germany,* Paris, 1972.

Paulsen, F., *German Education, Past and Present,* London, 1908.

Samuel, R. H. and Hinton Thomas, R., *Education and Society in Modern Germany,* London, 1949.

Simons, D., *Georg Kerschensteiner,* London, 1966.

Warren, R. L., *Education in Rebhausen,* New York, 1967.

Williams, G., *Apprenticeship in Europe,* London, 1963.

ARTICLES IN *WORLD YEARBOOK OF EDUCATION* (LONDON)

1966. *Church and State in Education.*
F. Hilker, Religion and the control of teachers: the case of Germany.
1967. *Educational Planning.*
F. Edding, Educational planning in Western Germany.
H. P. Widmaier, Educational planning in Western Germany: A Case Study.
1968. *Education within Industry.*
W. Niens, The historical and social background to education in West Germany.
S. A. Edenhofner, Training in the retail trades in the German Federal Republic.

157

1969. *Examinations.*
K. Ingenkamp, The organisation and structure of examinations in West Germany.
1970. *Education in Cities.*
G. Hausmann, A megalopolis: the Ruhr/Rhein complex.
1971/2. *Higher Education in a Changing World.*
D. Goldschmidt and S. Hübner, Changing concepts of the university in society: the West German case.
1972/3. *Universities Facing the Future.*
H. Hamm-Brücher, Towards the comprehensive university in Germany.

ARTICLES IN *COMPARATIVE EDUCATION* (OXFORD)

J. Lynch, A problem of status: teacher training in West Germany, vol. III, no. 3.
E. Schuppe, The State, problems and trends in the development of the West German educational system, vol. V, no. 2.
R. F. Lawson, The political foundations of German education, vol. VI, no. 3.
R. L. Merritt, E. P. Flerlage, and A. J. Merritt, Democratizing West German education, vol. VII, no. 3.
A. Hearnden, Inter-German relations and educational policy, vol. IX, no. 1.
M. Tournier, Women and access to university in France and Germany 1861–1967, vol. IX, no. 3.
A. Hearnden, Individual freedom and State intervention in East and West German education, vol. X, no. 2.
J. P. E. Hall, An alternative way to tertiary education: West Germany's *Fachoberschule,* vol. X, no. 2.

ARTICLES IN *COMPARATIVE EDUCATION REVIEW* (NEW YORK)

J. H. van de Graaff, West Germany's Abitur quota and school reform, vol. XI, no. 1.
S. B. Robinsohn and J. C. Kuhlmann, Two decades of non-reform in West German education, vol. XI, no. 3.
R. L. Merritt, E. P. Flerlage, and A. J. Merritt, Political man in postwar West German education, vol. XV, no. 3.
J. Lynch, The birth of a profession: German grammar school teachers and new humanism, vol. XV, no. 1.
M. Krueger and B. Wallisch-Prinz, University reform in West Germany, vol. XVI, no. 2.

ARTICLES IN *INTERNATIONAL REVIEW OF EDUCATION* (HAMBURG)

J. Huddleston, Trade union education in the Federal Republic of Germany: a survey and critical evaluation, vol. XIV, no. 1.
R. F. Lawson, A comparison of political attitudes among a sample of urban youth in West Germany and Canada, vol. XIX, no. 4.

Index

159

162 *Index*

SOME OTHER TITLES OF INTEREST

BENDING, C. W.
Communication and the Schools

BLAUG, M.
Economics of Education, 2nd edition

CROSS, G. R.
The Psychology of Learning

DAVIES, T. I.
School Organization

DIXON, K.
Philosophy of Education and the Curriculum

FLETCHER, B.
Universities in the Modern World

FRASER, W. R.
Residential Education

HALSALL, E.
Becoming Comprehensive: Case Histories

HALSALL, E.
The Comprehensive School: Guidelines for the Reorganization of Secondary Education

HENDERSON, J. L.
Education for World Understanding

HUGHES, M. G.
Secondary School Administration: A Management Approach, 2nd edition

HUGHES, P. M.
Guidance and Counselling in Schools

HUNTER, S. L.
The Scottish Educational System, 2nd edition

JESSOP, F. W.
Lifelong Learning

JOHNSTON, D. J.
Teachers' In-service Education

KELSALL, R. K. and KELSALL, H. M.
The Schoolteacher in England and the United States

KING, E. J.
Education and Social Change

163

KING, E. J.
The Teacher and the Needs of Society in Evolution

LEACH, R. J.
International Schools and Their Role in the Field of International Education

MOORE, W. G.
The Tutorial System and Its Future

SPOLTON, L.
The Upper Secondary School

WEARING KING, R.
The English Sixth-form College